Total Training
for
Young Champions

Total Training for Young Champions

TUDOR O. BOMPA, PhD

York University

Human Kinetics

Library of Congress Cataloging-in-Publication Data

Bompa, Tudor O.
    Total training for young champions / Tudor O. Bompa.
      p. cm
    Includes bibliographical references.
    ISBN 0-7360-0212-X
    1. Physical education for children. I. Title.
    GV443 .B62 2000
    613.7'042--dc21   99-046655

ISBN: 0-7360-0212-X

Acquisitions Editor: Martin Barnard
Developmental Editor: Cassandra Mitchell
Assistant Editors: Laura Majersky, Kim Thoren, and Wendy McLaughlin
Copyeditor: Danelle Eknes
Proofreader: Jim Burns
Indexer: Betty Frizzéll
Graphic Designer: Robert Reuther
Graphic Artist: Tara Welsch
Photo Editor: Clark Brooks
Cover Designer: Keith Blomberg
Photographer (cover): Tom Roberts
Photographer (interior): Tom Roberts
Illustrators: Titus Deak (line drawings) and Tom Roberts (Mac drawings)
Printer: Versa Press

Human Kinetics books are available at special discounts for bulk purchase. Special editions or book excerpts can also be created to specification. For details, contact the Special Sales Manager at Human Kinetics.

Printed in the United States of America   10 9 8 7 6 5 4 3 2 1

Human Kinetics
Web site: http://www.humankinetics.com/

United States: Human Kinetics, P.O. Box 5076, Champaign, IL 61825-5076
1-800-747-4457
e-mail: humank@hkusa.com

Canada: Human Kinetics, 475 Devonshire Road Unit 100, Windsor, ON N8Y 2L5
1-800-465-7301 (in Canada only)
e-mail: humank@hkcanada.com

Europe: Human Kinetics, P.O. Box IW14, Leeds LS16 6TR, United Kingdom
+44 (0) 113-278 1708
e-mail: humank@hkeurope.com

Australia: Human Kinetics, 57A Price Avenue, Lower Mitcham, South Australia 5062
(08) 82771555
e-mail: humank@hkaustralia.com

New Zealand: Human Kinetics, P.O. Box 105-231, Auckland Central
09-523-3462
e-mail: humank@hknewz.com

To my grandchildren Karina and Corey

Contents

Preface ix

Acknowledgments xi

Chapter 1 **Training Guidelines for Young Athletes**   **1**

Chapter 2 **Stages of Athletic Development**   **21**

Chapter 3 **Flexibility Training**   **31**

Chapter 4 **Motor Skills Training**   **43**

Chapter 5 **Speed Training**   **63**

Chapter 6 **Strength and Power Training**   **93**

Chapter 7 **Endurance Training**   **149**

Chapter 8 **Excelling in Competition**   **167**

Chapter 9 **Long-Term Training Plans**   **183**

Bibliography 199

Index 203

About the Author 211

Preface

Childhood represents the most physically active stage of human development. Children like to play games and participate in physical activity and sports, and they certainly love to compete.

Parents, instructors, coaches, and administrators search for the best training programs to increase children's athletic potential. Coaches often become role models, and children dream of surpassing the achievements of Michael Jordan, Kurt Browning, Joe Montana, Tara Lipinski, Carl Lewis, or Nadia Comaneci. It is, however, a grave mistake to submit children to the training programs of adults. After all, children are not simply little adults. Children are unique at each stage in their development, with differing physiological capabilities at each stage of growth. The physical and psychological changes (at times abrupt) that occur at each stage are accompanied by critical behavioral transformations. It is important for anyone working with children to be well informed regarding all the physical, emotional, and cognitive changes they go through during the development stages, and to structure training that is best suited for each stage.

Of the great number of books written on training, the majority refer to elite athletes, and few discuss training programs designed specifically for children. Along with many specialists and researchers on the specifics of training for young athletes, for 20 years I have gathered information and experience regarding the best possible approach to training children. The intent of *Total Training for Young Champions* is to bridge the gap between research and application, and between a hit-and-miss and a long-term approach to children's training.

From early childhood to maturation, people go through several stages of development, which include prepuberty, puberty, postpuberty, and maturation. For each development stage there is a corresponding phase of athletic training: initiation (prepuberty), athletic formation (puberty), specialization (postpuberty), and high performance (maturation). While each development stage roughly corresponds to a typical age range, it's important to understand that training programs must be designed according to the athlete's stage of maturation rather than chronological age because individual needs and demands vary with each athlete. Children of the same chronological age may differ by several years in their level of biological maturation. Moreover, while an early maturing child may show dramatic improvements initially, often a late maturer will be the better athlete in the long run. Therefore, it's important to look beyond the short-term achievements, and let children develop at their own pace.

The suggested training models in this book refer to the three major stages of development only: prepubescence, pubescence, and postpubescence. There are several books about maturation, specifically referring to the types of training to follow for each sport. Similarly, there are theory books that refer to high-performance training (please refer to Bompa, T.O., *Periodization: Theory and Methodology of Training*, 4ed. Champaign, Illinois, Human Kinetics, 1999).

The first two chapters of *Total Training for Young Champions* provide information about the anatomical, physiological, and psychological transformations children experience during the stages of growth and development. Chapters 3 through 7 discuss training for flexibility, coordination, speed, strength, and endurance, respectively. Each of these training chapters includes suggestions for structuring workouts, periodization models for each stage of development, and carefully illustrated exercises and games. Of the vast number of exercises for developing coordination, flexibility, speed, endurance, and strength, I have selected those that are most accessible and that anyone can perform without sophisticated machines. I also urge you to consider the suggested exercises and programs only as a guideline. As you become more familiar with the different training stages, you can add to or change any exercise or program to accommodate individual needs, specific training conditions, and environment.

Chapter 8 discusses when it is appropriate for young athletes to participate in organized competition, and ways parents and coaches can properly guide competition and training to ensure their athletes have a positive experience. The final chapter puts all of the previous chapters' information together in specific, long-term training plans for ten different sports.

A positive experience in sports and competition is key to ensuring children will enjoy an active lifestyle for years to come. Doing too much too soon, however, can result in overtraining or injury, and it may also lead children to lose interest and drop out of sports before ever fully developing their talents. A well-organized, long-term training program such as those presented here greatly increases the chance that athletes will stay with their sport and enjoy long-term excellence rather than short-term burnout. And that's what makes a champion athlete.

Acknowledgments

The preparation of this book could not have been possible without the contributions of several individuals who deserve my special recognition. I would like to extend my special thanks to Patricia Gallacher who used her talents to edit the original manuscript. Pat, your help has been tremendous and greatly appreciated. I have also been privileged to be associated with Titus Deac, whose talent enabled me to illustrate the exercises suggested in this book. Special thanks are also due to Martin Barnard, Cassandra Mitchell, Laura Majersky, and Wendy McLaughlin for their encouragement, guidance, and expertise in producing this book.

Training Guidelines for Young Athletes

Success in any arena is usually the result of planning, hard work, and commitment, and athletic training is no exception. All successful athletes are trained individuals who excel in a particular physical activity and usually have followed a well-designed, long-term training program over several years. In the field of sports, training is the process of repetitive, progressive exercises or work that improves the potential to achieve optimum performance. For athletes, this means long-term training programs that condition the body and mind to the specifics of competition and lead to excellence in performance.

Although many coaches and instructors are competent at designing seasonal training programs, it is essential to look beyond this short-term approach and plan for the athlete's long-term development. Proper athletic training should start in childhood, so the athlete can progressively and systematically develop body and mind to achieve long-term excellence rather than short-term burnout.

Far too often, the sports programs of children imitate programs of well-known elite athletes—those who, through their national or international achievements, have captivated the imaginations of young athletes and their coaches. Such programs are often imitated in detail, without evaluating the degree to which they serve the interests of young athletes. The followers of such programs often say that if the program worked for Michael Jordan, or Pete Sampras, it should work for my kids too! Coaches commonly employ these programs with little regard for the background and biological makeup of children and with no guiding concepts, such as training principles. Children are not just little adults, but have complex, distinct physiological characteristics that must be taken into account. This chapter discusses four training guidelines for young athletes.

Developing a Long-Term Training Program

For a long time, some coaches suggested that performing sport-specific exercises from an early age was the best way to develop an optimal training program. Some sport physiologists took this old concept, which some coaches still use today, and developed it into a principle of training. They suggested that to yield the fastest results a training program must do the following:

- Stress the energy system that is dominant in a given sport. For instance, a sprinter must do just sprints, and a long-distance athlete must train only the aerobic energy system.
- Follow motor skill specificity, meaning that athletes must select exercises that mimic the skill pattern and involve only the muscle groups they use to perform a technical skill.

The fact that laboratory research demonstrates that specificity training results in faster adaptation, leading to faster increments of performance, does not mean that coaches and athletes have to follow it from an early age to physical maturation.

This is the narrow approach applied to children's sports, in which the only scope of training is achieving quick results, irrespective of what may happen in the future of the young athlete. In their attempt to achieve the fast results, coaches expose children to highly specific and intensive training without taking the time to build a good base. This is like trying to build a high-rise building on a poor foundation. Obviously such a construction error will result in the collapse of the building. Likewise, encouraging athletes to narrowly focus on their development in one sport before they are ready physically and psychologically often leads to problems.

- It can lead to unilateral, narrow development of the muscles and organ functions.
- It can disturb the harmonious physical development and biological equilibrium, which are prerequisites of physical efficiency, athletic performance, and the development of a healthy person.
- Over the long term, it can result in overuse, overtraining, and even injuries.
- It can have a negative impact on the mental health of the children involved, because of the high stress levels this type of training creates and participation in many competitions.
- It can interfere with children's developing social relationships, such as failing to make friends outside sports, because of the many hours of activity associated with intensive training.
- It can affect the motivation of children, because the program can be too stressful, boring, and lacking in fun. Often young athletes may quit the sport

before they experience physiological and psychological maturation. Consequently, a young and talented person may never find out how talented he or she could have become.

Multilateral Development

It's important for young children to develop a variety of fundamental skills to help them become good general athletes *before* they start training in a specific sport. This is called multilateral development, and it is one of the most important training principles for children and youth.

Multilateral, or multiskill, development is common in Eastern European countries, where there are sport schools that offer a basic training program. Children who attend these schools develop fundamental skills, such as running, jumping, throwing, catching, tumbling, and balancing. The children become extremely well coordinated and acquire skills that are fundamental to success in a variety of individual and team sports, such as track and field, basketball, and soccer. Most programs also have a swimming component, as swimming helps children develop aerobic capacities while minimizing the physical stresses on their joints.

If we encourage children to develop a variety of skills, they will probably experience success in several sporting activities, and some will have the inclination and desire to specialize and develop their talents further. When children demonstrate interest in further developing their talent, we must provide the necessary guidance and opportunities. It takes years of training to become a world-class athlete, and we must provide those young athletes striving for excellence with a systematic, long-term plan based on sound, scientific principles.

Figure 1.1 illustrates the sequential approach to developing athletic talent over several years. Although the ages will vary from sport to sport, and from individual to individual, the model demonstrates the importance of progressive development. The base of the pyramid, which through analogy we may consider the foundation of any training program, consists of multilateral development. When the development reaches an acceptable level, athletes specialize in one specific sport and enter the second phase of development. The result will be high performance.

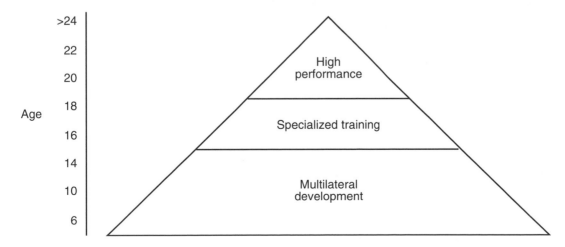

Figure 1.1 Suggested long-term approach to specificity of training.

Adapted, by permission, from T.O. Bompa, 1999, *Periodization training for sports* (Champaign, IL: Human Kinetics), 39.

The purpose of multilateral development is to improve overall adaptation. Children and youth who develop a variety of skills and motor abilities are more likely to adapt to demanding training loads, without experiencing stresses associated with early specialization. For example, young athletes who specialize in middle-distance running may be able to further develop their aerobic capacities by running, but they are also more susceptible to overuse injuries. Athletes who are capable of swimming, cycling, and running can exercise their cardiorespiratory systems in a variety of ways and significantly reduce the chance of injuries.

We should encourage young athletes to develop the skills and motor abilities they need for success in their chosen sport and other sports. For example, a well-rounded sports program for children and youth would include low-intensity exercises for developing aerobic capacity, anaerobic capacity, muscular endurance, strength, speed, power, agility, coordination, and flexibility.

A multilateral training program that focuses on overall athletic development, along with acquiring sport-specific skills and strategies, will lead to more successful performances at a later stage of development. As table 1.1 demonstrates, there are many benefits to a multilateral program. If we are interested in developing successful high-performance competitors, we must be prepared to delay specialization and sacrifice short-term results. The following two studies demonstrate this.

In a longitudinal study of 14 years performed in the former East Germany (Harre 1982), a large group of 9- to 12-year-old children were divided into two groups. The first group participated in a training program similar to the North American approach. This entailed early specialization in a given sport, using specificity exercises and training methods specific to the needs of the sport. The second group followed a generalized program in which the children participated in specific skills and physical training, along with a variety of other sports, skills, and overall physical training. The results, as table 1.1 illustrates, prove that a strong foundation leads to athletic success.

A Soviet survey (Nagorni 1978) reported similar findings. Among its conclusions, this longitudinal study reported the following:

Table 1.1	**Comparison Between Early Specialization and Multilateral Development**
Training philosophy	
Early specialization	**Multilateral program**
Quick performance improvement.	Slower performance improvement.
Best performance achieved at 15-16 years because of quick adaptation.	Best performance at 18 and older, the age of physiological and psychological maturation.
Inconsistency of performance in competitions.	Consistency of performance in competitions.
By age 18 many athletes were burned out and quit the sport.	Longer athletic life.
Prone to injuries because of forced adaptation.	Few injuries.

- The vast majority of the best Soviet athletes have had a strong multilateral foundation.

- Most athletes started to practice the sport at 7 or 8 years. During the first few years of activity all of them participated in various sports, such as soccer, cross-country skiing, running, skating, swimming, and cycling. From the age of 10 to 13 the children also experienced team sports, gymnastics, rowing, and track and field.

- Specialized programs started at 15 to 17 years, without neglecting sports and activities performed at earlier ages. Best performances were achieved after 5 to 8 years in the specialized sports.

- The athletes who specialized at a much earlier age had achieved their best performances at a junior age level. These performances were never duplicated when they became seniors (over 18 years). Quite a few had retired from sports before reaching senior levels. Only a minority of the athletes who specialized early on was able to improve performance at the senior age.

- Many top-class Soviet athletes had started to train in an organized environment at the junior age level (14 to 18). They never had been junior champions or held a national record. At the senior age, however, many achieved national- and international-class performances.

- Most athletes had considered that their success was possible and facilitated by the multilateral foundation they had built during childhood and junior age.

- The study concluded that specialization should not start before the age of 15 or 16 in most sports.

Although multilateral training is most important during the early stages of development, it should also be part of the training regimen for advanced athletes. Figure 1.2 illustrates that the ratio between multilateral development and specialized training changes significantly throughout the long-term training process. However, it is important for athletes to maintain the multilateral foundation they established during their early development throughout their athletic careers. Take for instance the case of Jane, a 12-year-old tennis player. Every week Jane engages in 10 hours of tennis and 4 to 5 hours of other physical and multilateral training such as flexibility, basic strength (using medicine balls and dumbbells), and agility exercises. A parent or a coach might feel that more tennis drills would make Jane a better-skilled player. However, increasing her tennis training is possible only at the expense of multilateral training. In the short term Jane may improve her tennis skills, but the lack of training in basic physical abilities such as strength, agility, and flexibility will thwart her playing abilities in the long term. When Jane is 18 her lack of good physical qualities would lower her overall tennis playing potential through weaker strokes, slower movement on the court, and decreased agility and quickness.

What figure 1.2 suggests is a long-term ratio between specific and multilateral development. The latter slightly decreases as Jane matures. If at the age of 12 Jane is doing 4 to 5 hours of multilateral training, at age 16 she might do 3.5 to 4 hours. At the same time her tennis-specific training may increase to 14 to 16 hours per week.

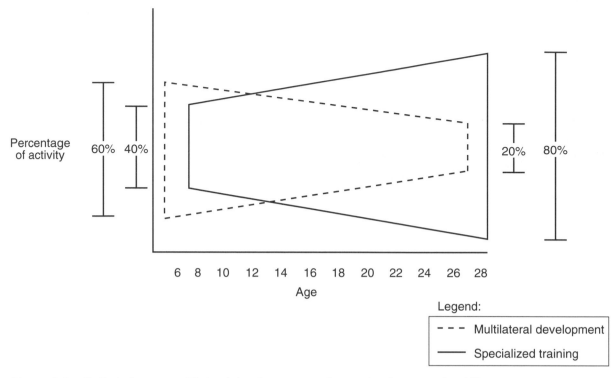

Figure 1.2 Ratio between multilateral development and specialized training for different ages.

Specialized Development

Specialization takes place after athletes have developed a solid multilateral foundation, and when they have the desire to specialize in a particular sport or position in a team sport. Specialization is necessary to achieve high performance in any sport because it leads to physical, technical, tactical, and psychological adaptation. It is a complex process. From the onset of specialization, athletes have to prepare for ongoing increments in training volume and intensity.

Once specialization takes place, training should include exercises that enhance development for the specific sport and exercises that develop general motor abilities. However, the ratio between the two forms of training varies considerably from sport to sport. For example, let us look at the difference between long-distance runners and high jumpers. The training volume for long-distance runners will consist mostly of running drills or activities, such as cycling and swimming, that enhance aerobic endurance. High jumpers will have a program consisting of approximately 40 percent specific high jumping drills and exercises, and 60 percent exercises such as plyometrics and weight training to develop particular motor abilities, for example, leg strength and jumping power.

As table 1.2 demonstrates, there are general ages that athletes should start developing skills and specializing in a specific sport, with the hope of eventually reaching a high-performance standard. It is important to understand, however, that even during the specialization stage of development, athletes should only contribute 60 to 80 percent of their total training time to performing exercises from a specialized sport. They should spend the balance of time on multilateral development and improving specific biomotor abilities.

Table 1.2	**Guidelines for the Road to Specialization**		
Sport	Age to begin practicing the sport	Age to start specialization	Age to reach high performance
Archery	12-14	16-18	23-30
Athletics			
Sprinting	10-12	14-16	22-26
Mid-distance run	13-14	16-17	22-26
Long-distance run	14-16	17-19	25-28
Jumps	12-14	16-18	22-25
Triple jumps	12-14	17-19	23-26
Long jumps	12-14	17-19	23-26
Throws	14-15	17-19	23-27
Badminton	10-12	14-16	20-25
Baseball	10-12	15-16	22-28
Basketball	10-12	14-16	22-28
Biathlon	10-13	16-17	23-26
Bobsled	12-14	17-18	22-26
Boxing	13-15	16-17	22-26
Canoeing	12-14	15-17	22-26
Continental handball	10-12	14-16	22-26
Cycling	12-15	16-18	22-28
Diving			
Women	6-8	9-11	14-18
Men	8-10	11-13	18-22
Equestrian	10-12	14-16	22-28
Fencing	10-12	14-16	20-25
Field hockey	11-13	14-16	20-25
Figure skating	7-9	11-13	18-25
Football	12-14	16-18	23-27
Gymnastics			
Women	6-8	9-10	14-18
Men	8-9	14-15	22-25
Ice hockey	6-8	13-14	22-28
Judo	8-10	15-16	22-26
Modern pentathlon	11-13	14-16	21-25
Rowing	11-14	16-18	22-25

(continued)

Sport	Age to begin practicing the sport	Age to start specialization	Age to reach high performance
Rugby	13-14	16-17	22-26
Sailing	10-12	14-16	22-30
Shooting	12-15	17-18	24-30
Skiing			
Alpine	7-8	12-14	18-25
Nordic (under 30K)	12-14	16-18	23-28
Over 30K	10-12	17-19	24-28
Jumping	—	14-15	22-26
Soccer	10-12	14-16	22-26
Speed skating	10-12	15-16	22-26
Squash/Handball	10-12	15-17	23-27
Swimming			
Women	7-9	11-13	18-22
Men	7-8	13-15	20-24
Synchronized swimming	6-8	12-14	19-23
Table tennis	8-9	13-14	22-25
Tennis			
Women	7-8	11-13	17-25
Men	7-8	12-14	22-27
Volleyball	10-12	15-16	22-26
Water polo	10-12	16-17	23-26
Weightlifting	14-15	17-18	23-27
Wrestling	11-13	17-19	24-27

Table 1.2 *(continued)*

Once athletes have decided to specialize, they must prepare to use specific training methods for adapting to the physical and psychological demands of the sport. The training demands increase significantly, formalized testing begins, and coaches plan and schedule organized competitions on a yearly basis.

Specialization takes place at different ages, depending on the sport. In sports that require artistry of movement, complex motor skill development, and a high degree of flexibility, such as gymnastics, diving, and figure skating, athletes should specialize at a young age. For sports in which speed and power dominate, such as football, baseball, and volleyball, athletes can start practicing the fundamental sport techniques at a young age. Specialization, however, should only take place once the athletes are capable of effectively coping with the demands of high-intensity training. In most speed and power sports, specialization should take place toward the end of the adolescent growth spurt. For other sports, such as long-distance running, cross-country skiing, and cycling, in which success depends on the ability to cope with maximal endurance efforts, athletes can specialize at the same time they develop speed and power, or later. Some endurance athletes are capable of achieving outstanding performance results at 30 years of age or older.

Adding Training Variety

Throughout the long process of developing champion athletes, children and youth experience thousands of hours of training and complete exercises and drills many thousands of times to develop their abilities. If training programs are not closely monitored and varied, many athletes will have difficulty coping with the physical and psychological stresses. Including diverse exercises and developing a range of skills in the training program at every stage of the developmental process not only helps athletes develop new abilities, but also prevents injury and avoids boredom and burnout.

Most team sports expose athletes to a variety of training methods. To strive for excellence in sports such as hockey, baseball, and basketball, athletes must become competent in many skills and exercises, which they develop most effectively through training diversity. In other sports, especially individual sports such as swimming and cycling, there is less diversity. For example, swimmers rarely participate in other sports and often perform the same exercises, technical elements, and drills 2 to 3 hours a day, 4 to 7 days a week, 45 to 50 weeks a year, for 20 years. This type of repetitive training may lead to overuse injuries and psychological problems, particularly the emotional difficulties associated with monotony and boredom.

To overcome these problems, coaches should be capable of incorporating a variety of exercises into each practice session. Using movements of similar technical patterns from other activities can enrich the list of drills coaches use. They can also include exercises that develop the motor abilities for the specific sport, such as speed, power, and endurance. For example, middle-distance runners who experience excessive muscular fatigue or overuse injuries may benefit more by completing an interval workout while running in the water than running on a hard track surface. Cross-country skiing will also help develop endurance, without placing the same strain on the joints of the legs. A coach who is creative and knowledgeable has a distinct advantage when designing workouts, because he or she can design each workout to use a variety of exercises and drills. If a coach can also periodically conduct a session away from the normal training environment, this will keep the young athletes stimulated, interested, and in some cases more motivated.

Coaches can also vary training sessions by having part of the practice, such as the warm-up, in a different environment or by doing the warm-up with athletes from other sports. For instance, football players can do their warm-up with track athletes, who have a more agile type of warm-up. Or, basketball players can warm up with middle-distance runners on the grass, where some interval training can also be performed (e.g., 6×60 seconds at 60 to 70 percent velocity, with an easy jog of 4 to 5 minutes between). Similarly, baseball players can warm up with track and field throwers, using medicine balls. It is also possible to design sessions during the off-season that encourage athletes to train particular motor abilities by participating in other sports. For example, distance runners could develop their endurance through cross-country skiing, cycling, or swimming.

Performing a variety of exercises also develops muscles other than those the athlete uses specifically in the chosen sport. Too much specificity training may result in overuse injuries. Moreover, it may cause imbalances between the agonistic muscles, the muscles specifically used in a sport—and the antagonistic ones (those which oppose to movement of the agonistic muscles). When there is a strong imbalance between these two sets of muscles, the pull of agonistic muscles is so strong that it may cause an injury at the tendons and muscle tissue level of the antagonistic muscles. Therefore, a variety of exercises using many muscles of the body can decrease the incidence of injury. Similarly, variations of movement, including practicing other sports, will improve coordination and agility. A well-coordinated and agile athlete will quickly learn difficult skills later.

Coaches who are creative and incorporate variety into their training programs will see the benefits. Athletes will remain highly motivated and be less likely to experience overuse injury.

Understanding Individual Characteristics

Every athlete is different with unique personalities, physical characteristics, social behaviors, and intellectual capacities. Under specific circumstances, the structure of an individual training program represents a means by which athletes are objectively and subjectively observed. To effectively design training programs for athletes, it is essential to understand their individual strengths and limitations. The limited working capacity of athletes varies significantly. The coach must consider individual differences, such as stage of development, training background and experience, health status, recovery rate between training sessions and following competitions, and gender particularities.

It is essential for us as coaches to cater to the individual needs of each athlete. It is no longer suitable, or acceptable, to categorize children and youth strictly based on chronological age, as children of the same age can differ by several years in their anatomical maturation. Considering anatomical age, biological age, and athletic age is crucial.

Anatomical Age

Anatomical age refers to the several stages of anatomical growth that we can recognize by identifying particular characteristics. Although there are many individual differences regarding characteristics, table 1.3 summarizes the particular development stages of children and youth.

Anatomical age clearly demonstrates the complexities of growth and development. It certainly helps explain why some children develop skills and motor abilities faster or slower than others do. A child who is better developed anatomically will learn many skills faster than a child who is less developed. Although many children follow similar growth patterns, there are variations. For example, climate, latitude, terrain (mountainous versus flat), and living environment (urban versus rural) can significantly affect the rate at which youth develop. For instance, children in hot climate countries are maturing much faster sexually, emotionally, and physically. As a result, athletic performance can increase faster

Phase of development	Chronological age (years)	Stage	Age	Developmental characteristics
Early childhood	0-2	Newborn Infant Crawling Walking	0-30 days 1-8 months 9-12 months 1-2 years	Fast organ development.
Preschool	3-5	Small Medium Big	3-4 years 4-5 years 5-6 years	A stage of unequal rhythm of development when important and complex changes occur (functional, behavioral, personality).
School years	6-18	Prepuberty	6-11 (girls) 7-12 (boys)	A slow and balanced development when the functions of some organs become more efficient.
		Puberty	11-13 (girls) 12-14 (boys)	Fast growth and development in height, weight, and the efficiency of some organs; sexual maturation with change in interests and behaviors.
		Postpuberty Adolescence	13-18 (girls) 14-18 (boys)	A slow, balanced, and proportional development; functional maturation.
Young adult	19-25	Maturity	19-25 years	Maturation period doubled by perfecting all functions and psychological traits. Athletic and psychological potentials are maximized.

Table 1.3 **Stages of Anatomical Age**

at the age of 14 to 18 than in countries of colder climates. Similarly, children living at high altitudes tend to be more effective in endurance sports than their low altitude counterparts. The runners from Kenya, for example, dominate distance running in track and field. Living at a high altitude for generations, where oxygen is in lower proportions than at sea level, has made these individuals adjust to scarce oxygen. Consequently, they have superior genetics for endurance—they use oxygen more effectively, giving them an advantage over athletes coming from low plains.

From the perspective of athletic development, the third phase (16 to 18 years) is the most important. During this phase, athletes may be at many different levels. In some sports they will be developing a variety of skills and motor abilities, and establishing a foundation for future development. In other sports such as gymnastics, athletes will be maximizing their performances.

During the latter part of the school years, many athletes who have developed a solid foundation and desire to pursue excellence in a particular sport will be able to specialize.

Biological Age

Biological age refers to the physiological development of the organs and systems in the body that help determine the physiological potential, both in training and

© Rob Tringali/Sports Chrome

competition, to reach a high-performance level. When categorizing and selecting athletes, you must consider biological age. A rigid chronological age classification system in sports will frequently result in misjudgments, faulty evaluations, and poor decisions.

Two athletic children with the same anatomical age, who look the same anatomically in height, weight, and muscular development, could be of different biological age and possess different abilities to perform a training task. A tall, strong-looking child is not necessarily your faster athlete. On the contrary, especially in team sports, a slightly smaller youngster may be more agile in certain positions on your team. While anatomical age is visible, the biological age development is not. The heart's efficiency, the effectiveness of oxygen utilization, is hidden from the naked eye. A less impressive physique may hide a powerful and efficient heart, which is so important in endurance sports. This is why you must assess biological age objectively through simple tests, to find the difference in training potential between children.

Without considering biological age, it is difficult to determine whether certain children are too young to perform particular skills or to tolerate specific training loads. It is also difficult to assess the potential of older athletes, who many might consider to be too old to achieve high performance.

Unfortunately, in many sports programs, coaches still use chronological age as the major criteria for classification. For example, many studies have demonstrated that children born in December are less likely to experience success in sports programs than those who were born in January. In many cases, when divisions are determined by chronological age, children born in the same calendar year are in the same category. As a result, children born early in the year will likely have an anatomical and biological advantage over children born in December.

It is important for us to consider individual differences in biological age. The following list will illustrate some tremendous differences in biological age of international sport champions:

- Murray Wood, from Australia, was an Olympic silver medalist for rowing in 1956 at the age of 39.
- At the 1964 Olympic Games in Tokyo, M. Takemoto, from Japan, received a silver medal in gymnastics at the age of 44.
- At the 1976 Montreal Olympic Games, Nadia Comaneci, a 14-year-old from Romania, won the gold medal in artistic gymnastics.
- L. Ceapura, from Romania, received a silver medal in rowing at the 1980 Moscow Olympic Games at the age of 39.
- In 1988, 15-year-old Allison Higson, from Canada, broke the world record in the 100-meter breaststroke.
- In 1991, 12-year-old A. Yeu, from China, was a world champion in diving.
- Gordie Howe, from Canada, was still playing hockey in the National Hockey League at the age of 52 (from 1946-1971 and 1979-1980).

This list, which represents only a small percentage of the athletes who have achieved remarkable performances in sports, demonstrates the different biological potentials at various chronological ages.

Athletic Age

Coaches often determine anatomical age and biological age subjectively because of the difficulty in conducting accurate assessments. As a result, it is difficult to determine when children and youth are ready to participate in high-caliber competitions. Many national and international sports organizations have closely examined scientific research regarding biological potential at a given age. Although there is often controversy concerning specific decisions, many organizations have stipulated minimum age requirements for competition. In table 1.4, I present some minimum ages for international competitions, such as world championships or the Olympic Games.

Athletic age, especially the minimum age and the designated age for senior-level competition, has important implications on the design of long-term training plans. Training programs have to be structured so the focus for children and youth, in most sports, is on overall development and not early specialization. If we focus on developing athletes over several years, we will likely produce some great international champions.

Table 1.4	Ages for Participation in International Competitions		
Sport	Minimum age	Designated ages	
		Junior	Senior
Track and field	14	18	>19
Boxing	—	18	>19
Canoeing	—	19	>20
Diving	14	—	—
Equestrian	—	18	>19
Fencing	—	20	>21
Gymnastics	14		
Women	—	18	>19
Men			
Ice hockey	—	18	>21
Modern pentathlon	16	19	>20
Rowing	16	18	>19
Skiing (Nordic)	—	19	>20
Swimming	—	15	>16
Tennis	—	18	>19
Volleyball	—	18	>19
Weightlifting	16	19	>20

© Joanna Gleason Photography

Increasing Training Load Appropriately

Understanding the methods used to increase training load is essential for any good training program. The amount that children and youth will improve their physical abilities in a particular sport is the direct result of the amount and quality of work they achieve in training. From the early stages of development through the high-performance level, athletes must increase the workload in training gradually, according to their individual needs.

Athletes who develop gradually will likely be more capable of performing work over a long period. During adaptation to a particular training load, athletes increase their capacities to cope with the stresses and demands of training and competition.

The rate at which young athletes improve their performance depends on the rate and method they use to increase the training load. If they maintain the load at approximately the same level for a long time (standard load), improvements in performance are barely visible. If they increase the load too much, some immediate benefits may be visible, but they substantially increase the likelihood of injuries. It is important, therefore, for young athletes to slowly increase the training load. Although immediate short-term results will be difficult to attain, the long-term potential for performance is much greater.

During the early stages of development it is difficult to monitor training loads, because performance improvements in strength, speed, and endurance for some young athletes may be the result of normal growth and development. However, it is important to progressively increase training loads. Athletes 10 to 15 years of age who participate on a baseball team that practices twice a week and plays a game each weekend all season (standard load) will not likely experience significant improvements during the season as a result of training. They may improve as a result of their growth and development, but without an increase in the overall training volume, it will be difficult to further develop baseball skills and specific motor abilities. You can progressively increase training programs for young, developing athletes in the following areas.

Duration of Training Sessions

The length of each training session can increase from the beginning of the season to the end, for example, from one hour to two hours, as table 1.5 suggests.

As the duration increases to 1 hour and 30 minutes, it is important to keep the children's interest up by having training variety, and to have longer rest intervals between drills and exercises, so the children may more easily cope with fatigue.

Note: A training session performed in *hot* and *humid* conditions should always be much shorter because children become fatigued faster.

Number of Exercises

As part of the strategy to progressively increase the training load, athletes can also expand the number of exercises and drills they perform per training session over the weeks and years. The increased number of repetitions of technical drills or exercises for physical development will certainly improve the athletes' performance. I have to mention again that, as the number of exercises and drills increase, the instructor must carefully monitor the rest interval between them. Longer rest intervals will give children more energy to perform all the work planned for that training session.

Frequency of Training Sessions

To constantly and progressively challenge the bodies of young athletes toward performance improvement, you must regularly increase the frequency, or number of training sessions per week.

This is essential because skills develop during training sessions and not during the games and competitions. For young athletes to constantly master the skills of the sport and develop the motor abilities for future competitions, they must have more training sessions than games. Therefore, parents should require that instructors and coaches, especially in the team sports, have a ratio of two to four training sessions to one game. Such an approach will pay off later in an athletic career, because athletes will properly acquire skill fundamentals at the ideal age.

Table 1.5	**Progression of Training Session Length for a Soccer Team**				
Month	April	May	June	July	August
Duration of sessions in hours	1	1:15	1:30	1:30	Off

Weeks of Training

Coaches who extend their season so there are more weeks of preparation before competitions begin will likely see results. This is true more for individual sports, such as track and field and swimming, than for team sports. Often in soccer, baseball, football, and so on, children experience few weeks of training before games start.

The ideal situation is to practice for most months of the year, as this will lead to better development of skills and motor abilities. The coach or parent can take advantage of a long preseason training to work with the athletes on skill acquisition while there is no pressure of games to play during the weekend.

If coaches and instructors cannot organize such a training program, parents should do so. The basement, garage, an open field, or the backyard are all great places for training simple skills, and especially motor abilities. To develop basic strength or endurance you do not need the most sophisticated facilities.

Months of Training

Young children may only commit a few months to practicing a specific sport, and often these are the months of the competitive season. As young athletes become older and more experienced, however, they should commit more months to training in a specific sport if they desire high-performance results. When young athletes make the commitment to specialize in a particular sport, they will likely be training 10 months or more a year.

I can also suggest a progression within these areas. At first, increase the duration of training from two times a week at 1 hour, to two times a week at 1 hour and 15 minutes, then to two times a week at 1 hour and 30 minutes. If you consider this the upper level of the child's tolerance, then you can increase the frequency of training sessions per week from two times at 1 hour and 30 minutes, to three times at 1 hour and 30 minutes. In a later stage of developing the athlete's potential, you can increase the frequency to four or five training sessions per week and, for some sports, an even higher number.

As the frequency reaches an upper limit for that development stage (i.e., three times at 1 hour and 30 minutes), you can now increase the number of exercises and drills per training session. There are two methods to consider:

1. Increase the number of exercises before taking rest (i.e., from one set of 8, to one set of 10, 12, or even 14 ball passes, drills, or exercises).
2. Decrease the rest interval between sets (i.e., from 2 minutes to 1.5 minutes and later to 1 minute).

Step Loading

It is important to progressively increase training loads, because athletes who experience standard loads, even at a young age, will likely stop improving. The most effective way to increase the training load is to understand and use the *step method*. With this method, increase the load for two or three weeks; then decrease it for one week to allow regeneration, or recovery. Figures 1.3 and 1.4 illustrate two options. I suggest the first option for young children, and I

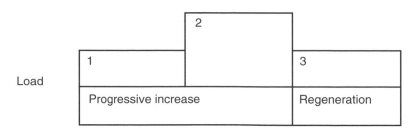

Figure 1.3   Increase of training load for a three-week cycle.

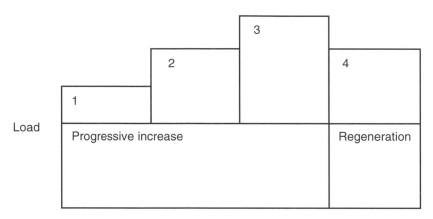

Figure 1.4   Increase of training load for a four-week cycle.

recommend the second model for athletes in their late teens and young athletes who are advanced in a particular sport. Both models refer to the training weeks when athletes are not in competitions.

As figure 1.3 suggests, increase the training load progressively. During the first two steps, each representing a week, the increased load challenges young athletes to adapt to a greater amount of work. As they become fatigued, slightly decrease the load in week 3 to allow recovery before further increasing the training load.

As figure 1.4 demonstrates, we expect athletes in their late teens and advanced young athletes to cope with a more challenging program. During the first three weeks of training, increase the load from week to week, which leads to higher adaptation levels and, ultimately, superior performances. We assume that by the end of the third step, the fatigue level will be high, so again slightly decrease the load in step 4 to allow recovery. To continue increasing the training load after the third week will result in greater fatigue, which may lead to a critical level of fatigue or, over time, to overtraining. If you do not incorporate a regeneration week into the training plan when athletes are experiencing fatigue, some may get injured, and they may lose interest in training and eventually drop out.

Table 1.6 offers suggestions regarding the training elements that you can use to increase the load from step to step, or to decrease it for the regeneration week of the four-week cycle. Table 1.6 does not exhaust all the training elements. For instance, you must increase others, such as distance, speed, or the number of drills and repetitions, in the same fashion.

Please note that in table 1.6 the number of training sessions peaks to four in step 3. If you use the three-week step method for children (figure 1.3), then the progression may be two for the first step and three for the second step. The number of hours of training increases in the same way. Regarding the rest interval, *standard* means the normal periods the instructor uses. After step 3 (figure 1.4) and step 2 (figure 1.3), use a slightly shorter rest period so the bodies of the young athletes are further challenged.

The regeneration week is crucial to the step method. At the end of the highest step, the athletes are tired, and to continue training at the same level of demand is a mistake. For the well-being of the young athletes, decrease the demand in training during this week. This will remove fatigue from the body, relax the mind, and replenish overall energy. Toward the end of this week, the athletes will feel rested and in a good mood for a further one or two weeks of increased load increments.

Table 1.6	How Training Elements Increase in the Step Method			
Training elements	Step 1	Step 2	Step 3	Step 4
Number of training sessions	2/3	3	4	3
Number of hours per training session	1:15	1:30	1:30 - 2:00	1:15 - 1:30
Rest interval between sets of drills or exercises	Standard	Standard	Shorter	Standard

As the regeneration week ends the step method can be applied again but at a slightly higher training demand. At the beginning of the preseason phase you can use a 5 to 10 percent increment in the workload. As the athletes adjust to this workload, especially in the second part of the preseason phase, the load increment from step to step can be increased by 10 to 20 percent.

As already mentioned, the step method is most valid during preseason, when the athletes train for upcoming competitions. It is not valid during the season of competitions, especially for team sports, when athletes play games at the end of the week. During the season, therefore, the load of training per week is steady, and you will organize a regeneration period to remove fatigue following a game. Athletes perform most training during the middle of the week and plan light training for the one day (or maximum of two days) before a game, so they will not experience fatigue that could impair a good performance (table 1.7).

Certainly there are other options for organizing the weekly program. A coach may organize only two training sessions a week, say Tuesday and Thursday, each one of steady intensity. Each session may, however, be of lighter intensity if the children look tired. Remember that rested children always play better games.

Training young athletes must be viewed as a long-term proposition where the load increments and overall physical, technical-tactical, and mental demands are applied gradually during the stages of growth and development.

Laying the foundation of sound training during childhood through multilateral development, rather than narrow, sport-specific training, will give your young athlete a better foundation for high performance. Variety in training, accounting for individual differences among athletes, and appropriately planning the load progression from stage to stage will also result in a more effective training program.

Table 1.7	Structure of Training per Week During the Season					
Monday	Tuesday	Wednesday	Thursday	Friday	Saturday	Sunday
Off	Light training	Intense training	Intense training	Light	Game training	Off

Chapter 2 discusses how to apply the concepts in this chapter to the three stages of children's athletic development—initiation, athletic formation, and specialization. The physical and emotional characteristics of each stage largely dictate a young athlete's training potential and therefore must be taken into account when designing a training program.

Stages of Athletic Development

Sport scientists and coaches claim that athletes who, as children and youths, experienced well-organized and systematic training programs usually accomplish the best performances. Impatient coaches that pressure children to achieve quick results usually fail, because the athletes often quit before attaining athletic maturation. By employing correct training principles discussed in chapter 1, and by dividing the training of children and youth into systematic stages of development, with clearly defined objectives, we will more likely produce healthy and outstanding athletes.

It is important, however, to keep in mind that children evolve at different rates. The growth rate of their bones, muscles, organs, and nervous systems are different from stage to stage, and these developments largely dictate their physiological and performance capabilities. This is why a training program *must* consider individual differences and training potential. Even in a team sport with, say, 14-year-old players, the differences between the players may be so great that some have the athletic potential of 16-year-olds (early developers), whereas others have only the physical capabilities of 12-year-old children (late developers). To neglect such large differences could mean that an early developer might be undertrained, whereas the late developer is overstressed.

A gradual, progressive program with no abrupt increases in intensities greatly increases training efficiency and reduces the chance of frustration and injury. This process is called *periodization of long-term training.* The term periodization is derived from the word period, meaning a certain time or phase of training. In connection with the topic of this book, periodization is the process of dividing training programs of all athletes, from entry level to elite class, into small segments of time, or short phases, so training is more effective. Periodization also refers to the long-term progression of the motor abilities necessary for an athlete to excel in the sport of his or her choice. In short, periodization represents a holistic approach to athletic development, including training, psychological, and sociological factors. Comprehensive periodization models for several sports are provided at the end of chapter 9, "Long-Term Training Plans".

It is essential for anyone involved in children's sports to incorporate periodization principles into their training. Figure 2.1 demonstrates that all athletes, regardless of their high-performance potential, should participate in a *multilateral* and a *specialized* phase of training. The concepts discussed in chapter 1 have to be applied now to the specifics of the physical and mental characteristics of each stage of development discussed below. The effectiveness of a training program and the workload planned in training must carefully regard these characteristics. The athletic potential of a child is strictly dependent on his physical and mental development. To disregard that means discomfort, stress, and even the possibility of injuring the young athlete. Within the multilateral phase, gradually introduce athletes to sport-specific training (initiation), and progressively form their athletic talents (athletic formation). The primary purpose of the multilateral phase is to build the foundation upon which the athlete can effectively develop complex motor abilities, resulting in a smooth transition to the specialized phase.

There are two stages within the specialized phase, namely *specialization* and *high performance*. During the specialization stage, athletes choose which sport and which position in the chosen sport they would like to play. Once athletes begin to specialize, the intensity and volume of training can increase progressively, and you can individualize conditioning programs. The final stage focuses on high performance in the chosen sport.

While figure 2.1 outlines ages associated with each stage, it is important to understand that this model can shift considerably depending on the sport. For

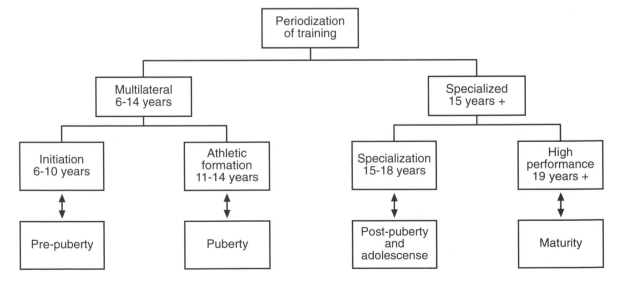

Figure 2.1   Periodization of long-term training.

Adapted, by permission, from T.O. Bompa, 1999, *Periodization: Theory and methodology of training.* (Champaign, IL: Human Kinetics), 258.

example, in sports such as women's gymnastics and diving, the age at each stage may be two to four years younger. It is also critical to understand that the rate at which children develop is highly varied, and you must consider the maturation differences of each athlete. The training programs in this book are based on the average rate of growth and development of a typical young athlete. Although the training guidelines and the suggested programs refer to chronological age, you should apply them according to the specific characteristics of your young athlete. In other words, in setting a training program for a group of children, you should consider their state of readiness for that kind of work instead of chronological age, and adjust training and competitive programs accordingly. Familiarity with the physical, mental, and social characteristics of athletes in the initiation, athletic formation, and specialization development stages will allow you to establish a training program that will enhance athlete development, resulting in high performance.

Initiation Stage—6 to 10 Years Old

Children in the initiation stage should participate in low-intensity training programs, in which the emphasis is fun. Most young children are not capable of coping with the physical and psychological demands of high-intensity training or organized competitions. Training programs for these young athletes must focus on overall athletic development and not sport-specific performance.

The body is growing at a steady rate and larger muscle groups are more developed than smaller ones. The cardiorespiratory system is developing and aerobic capacity is adequate for most activities. Anaerobic capacities, however, are limited at this stage as children have low tolerance to lactic acid accumulation. Body tissues are susceptible to injury. Ligaments are becoming stronger, but the bone ends are still cartilaginous and calcifying.

Attention span is short at this age and children are action oriented, thus they cannot sit and listen for long periods of time. It is especially important for training at this stage to be varied and creative. Participation and fun should be emphasized over winning.

The following guidelines will help in designing training programs that are suitable for young athletes in this stage:

- Emphasize multilateral development by introducing a wide variety of skills and exercises including running, jumping, catching, throwing, batting, balancing, and rolling.
- Provide every child with enough time to adequately develop skills and equal playing time in games and activities.
- Positively reinforce children who are committed and self-disciplined. Reinforce improvements in skill development.
- Encourage children to develop flexibility, coordination, and balance.
- Encourage children to develop various motor abilities in low-intensity environments. For example, swimming is a terrific environment for developing the cardiorespiratory system, while minimizing the stresses on joints, ligaments, and connective tissues.
- Select a suitable number of repetitions for each skill, and encourage children to perform each technique correctly.

- Modify the equipment and playing environment to a suitable level. For example, children do not have the strength to shoot an adult-size basketball into a 10-foot-high (3 meters) basket using the correct technique. The ball should be smaller and lighter and the basket should be lower.

- Design drills, games, and activities so children have opportunities for maximum active participation.

- Promote experiential learning by providing children with opportunities to design their drills, games, and activities. Encourage them to be creative and use their imaginations.

- Simplify or modify rules so children understand the game.

- Introduce modified games that emphasize basic tactics and strategies. For example, if children have developed basic individual skills such as running, dribbling a ball with the feet, and kicking a ball, they will likely be ready to successfully play a modified game of soccer. During the game, you could introduce the young athletes to situations that demonstrate the importance of teamwork and position play.

- Encourage children to participate in drills that develop attention control to prepare them for the greater demands of training and competition that occur in the athletic formation stage of development.

© Joanna Gleason Photography

- Emphasize the importance of ethics and fair play.
- Provide opportunities for boys and girls to participate together.
- Make sure that *sports are fun*.
- Encourage participation in as many sports as possible.

Athletic Formation—11 to 14 Years Old

It is appropriate to moderately increase the intensity of training during the athletic formation stage of development. Although most athletes are still vulnerable to injuries, their bodies and capacities are rapidly developing. Their cardiorespiratory system continues to develop, and tolerance to lactic acid accumulation is gradually improving.

It is important to understand that the variances in performance may be the result of differences in growth. Some athletes may be experiencing a rapid growth spurt, which can explain why they lack coordination during particular drills. As a result, emphasize developing skills and motor abilities, and not performing and winning.

The following guidelines will help you design training programs that are appropriate for the athletic formation stage.

- Encourage participation in a variety of exercises from the specific sport and from other sports, which will help them improve their multilateral base and prepare them for competition in their selected sport. Progressively increase the volume and intensity of training.
- Design drills that introduce athletes to fundamental tactics and strategies, and reinforce skill development.
- Help athletes refine and automate the basic skills they learned during the initiation stage and learn skills that are a little more complex.
- Emphasize improving flexibility, coordination, and balance.
- Emphasize ethics and fair play during training sessions and competitions.
- Provide all children with opportunities to participate at a challenging level.
- Introduce the athletes to exercises that develop general strength. The foundation for future strength and power gains should begin in this stage. Emphasize developing the core sections of the body, in particular the hips, lower back, and abdomen, as well as muscles at the extremities—shoulder joints, arms, and legs. Most exercises should involve body weight and light equipment, such as medicine balls and light dumbbells.
- Continue developing aerobic capacity. A solid endurance base will enable athletes to cope more effectively with the demands of training and competition during the specialization stage.
- Introduce athletes to moderate anaerobic training. This will help them adapt to high-intensity anaerobic training, which takes on greater importance in most sports during the specialization stage. Athletes should not compete in events that place excessive stress on the anaerobic lactic acid energy system, such as the 200-meter sprint and 400-meter dash in track and field. They are usually better suited for short sprints of less than 80 meters (87 yards), which involve the anaerobic lactic energy system, and endurance events that are longer distances at slower speeds, such as the 800 meters (870 yards) and longer, which test their aerobic capacities.

- Avoid competitions that place too much stress on the body anatomically. For example, most young athletes do not have sufficient muscular development to perform a triple jump with the correct technique. As a result, some may experience compression injuries from the shock which the body must absorb somewhere during the stepping and hopping segments of the jump.

- To improve concentration, introduce athletes to more complex drills. Encourage them to develop strategies for self-regulation and visualization. Introduce formalized mental training.

- Introduce athletes to a variety of fun competitive situations that allow them to apply various techniques and tactics. Young athletes like to compete; however, it is important to de-emphasize winning. Structure competitions to reinforce skill development. For example, you can base the objective of a javelin throwing competition on accuracy and technique rather than how far athletes can throw the javelin.

- Provide time for play and socializing with peers.

Specialization—15 to 18 Years Old

Athletes in the specialization stage are capable of tolerating greater training and competition demands than those in earlier stages. The most significant changes in training take place during this stage. Athletes who have been participating in a well-rounded program emphasizing multilateral development will now start performing more exercises and drills aimed specifically at high-performance development in one sport. Closely monitor the volume and intensity of training to ensure that athletes improve dramatically with little risk of injury. Toward the end of this athletic development stage, the athletes should have no major technical problems. Thus, the coach can move from a teaching to a coaching (training) role.

The following guidelines will help in designing training programs that are suitable for athletes who specialize in a particular sport.

- Closely monitor the development of athletes during this stage. They will be developing strategies for coping with the increased physical and psychological demands of training and competition. They are also vulnerable to experiencing physical and psychological difficulties from overtraining.

- Check for progressive improvements in the dominant motor abilities for the sport, such as power, anaerobic capacity, specific coordination, and dynamic flexibility.

- Increase the training volume for specific exercises and drills to facilitate a performance improvement. The body must adapt to specific training load increments to effectively prepare for competition; therefore, now is the time to stress specificity.

- Then, increase training intensity more rapidly than the volume, although you must still increase volume progressively. Prepare athletes to perform a particular skill, exercise, or drill with the appropriate rhythm and speed. Training should closely simulate the actions that take place during competitions. Although fatigue is a normal outcome of high-intensity training, it is important that athletes do not reach the state of exhaustion.

- Involve athletes in the decision-making process whenever possible.
- Continue to emphasize multilateral training, particularly during the pre-season. However, it is more important to emphasize specificity and to use training methods and techniques that will develop a high level of sport-specific efficiency, particularly during the competitive season.
- Encourage athletes to become familiar with the theoretical aspects of training.
- Emphasize exercising the muscles that athletes primarily use when performing technical skills (prime movers). Strength development should start to reflect the specific needs of the sport. Athletes who are weight training can start performing exercises that require fewer repetitions and a heavier weight. Avoid maximum strength training, in which athletes perform fewer than four repetitions of an exercise, particularly for those who are still growing.
- Make developing the aerobic capacity a high priority for all athletes, particularly those who participate in endurance or endurance-related sports.
- Progressively increase the volume and intensity of anaerobic training. Athletes are capable of coping with lactic acid accumulation.

© Claus Andersen

- Improve and perfect the techniques of the sport. Select specific exercises that will ensure the athletes are performing the skills in a manner that is biomechanically correct and physiologically efficient. Athletes should perform difficult technical skills frequently during training sessions, incorporate them into specific tactical drills, and apply them in competitions.
- Improve individual and team tactics. Incorporate game-specific drills into tactical training sessions. Select drills that are interesting, challenging, and stimulating, and that require quick decisions, fast actions, prolonged concentration, and a high level of motivation from the athletes. Athletes should demonstrate initiative, self-control, competitive vigor, and ethics and fair play in competitive situations.
- Increase the number of competitions progressively, so by the end of this stage the athletes are competing as frequently as senior-level competitors. It is also important to set objectives for competitions that focus on developing specific skills, tactics, and motor abilities. Although winning becomes increasingly important, do not overemphasize it.
- Athletes should practice mental training. Structure drills and exercises that develop concentration, attention control, positive thinking, self-regulation, visualization, and motivation to enhance sport-specific performance.

High Performance— 19 Years Old and Over

A well-designed training plan based on sound principles of long-term development will lead to high performance. Exceptional performance results that athletes achieved during the initiation, athletic formation, or specialization stages do not correlate with high-performance results as a senior competitor. As table 2.1 demonstrates, the majority of athletes are most successful after they have reached athletic maturation.

This book will be concerned only with the first three development stages. For further information on training for high performance, the reader may consider the following books, written by the same author:

- *Periodization: Theory and Methodology of Training,* 4th ed., Champaign, IL: Human Kinetics, 1999.
- *Periodization Training for Sports,* Champaign, IL: Human Kinetics, 1999.

The following chapters discuss methods and specific programs for the development of flexibility, motor skills, speed, strength, and endurance. Please observe that for each I apply a long-term progression in the difficulty of training and exercises. Please consider my suggestions discretely and apply them according to your training environment and the individual characteristics of your athletes.

Table 2.1	Average Age of Participants at the Olympic Games Between 1968 and 1992	
Sport	**Average age**
Athletics	24.1
Basketball	24.7
Boxing	22.7
Canoeing	24.2
Cycling	23.4
Equestrian	31.2
Fencing	24.1
Field hockey (men)	25.4
Gymnastics (women)	17.2
Gymnastics (men)	22.6
Judo	24.0
Rowing	24.2
Sailing	30.3
Shooting	33.2
Soccer	24.1
Swimming (women)	18.9
Swimming (men)	21.6
Volleyball (men)	25.2
Water polo (men)	25.3
Wrestling	24.8

chapter 3

Flexibility Training

Flexibility refers to the range of motion around a joint. Improving flexibility is a fundamental element of a young athlete's training program, as good flexibility enables the athlete to perform various movements and skills easily and helps prevent injury.

The ability to perform many movements and skills successfully depends on the range of motion, which has to be greater than the skills of the sport require. For instance, to hit a high ball during a soccer game, players have to lift their leg to the chest level, so they must be flexibile enough to go beyond that level. If they don't have that flexibility, they won't be able to learn and perfect the various movements required of the sport.

Flexibility training is also an injury-prevention strategy. Most sports involve repetitive movement, often through a limited range of motion, such as running. This can lead to muscle tightness and possibly muscle strains and tears. An immediate, careful, and progressively increased flexibility program will stretch the muscles, relieving muscle tightness and helping prevent injury. Developing flexibility, therefore, means not only meeting the needs of the sport, but also exceeding the range of motion normally required in the sport and developing a flexibility reserve to prevent injury.

The best time to perform stretching exercises is at the end of a general warm-up (jogging and calisthenics), during the rest interval between exercises, and at the end of the training session.

Developing Flexibility

Young children are flexible, but flexibility performance often decreases with age after puberty, especially for boys, presumably because of gains in muscle size, stature, and muscle strength. Flexibility therefore requires training throughout the stages of a young athlete's development. Because athletes can more easily develop flexibility at a young age, it has to be part of the training program for each young athlete, irrespective of sport specialization. Once they achieve the desired degree of flexibility, their objective for the flexibility program is to maintain that level. Maintenance is important year-round, as athletes quickly lose flexibility with inactivity, and reduced flexibility can make them prone to injury.

The initiation stage is therefore the ideal time for starting a good program to develop flexibility. Emphasize overall flexibility that involves all the joints of the body, because this will result in good basic development. This is important because specialization does not occur until later stages of athletic development, and no one knows which muscles will require the most flexibility as a result of training for a specific sport.

As boys start to build stronger muscles and grow in size, they begin to show some decline in flexibility, reaching the lowest level in the second part of pubescence. At the same time, girls continue to perform well. Puberty is the development stage when gender differences in flexibility are the largest.

During postpuberty, the trend of gender differences continues. Girls still show better flexibility than boys, although the difference is not as large as during puberty. As girls approach adolescence, however, they seem to reach a plateau (Docherty and Bell, 1985), which might maintain or even decrease during maturity. This is why overall flexibility training should be a constant concern for everyone involved in athletics.

Methods of Stretching

The best way to improve flexibility is to perform stretching exercises. There are three methods of performing stretching exercises: statically, ballistically, and using proprioceptive neuromuscular facilitation (PNF).

Before briefly exploring each method, it is important to mention that there exists some contradiction regarding which method is most efficient. Many coaches and athletes prefer the static method, fearing that the ballistic method may lead to muscle pulls. Although PNF has some limitations in its application it is often the preferred method.

Static stretching involves stretching to the limit of motion without forcing the stretch and holding the position without movement for a given time. Throughout the performance of static flexibility, the athlete should attempt to relax the muscles to achieve the maximum range of motion.

For both the static and PNF methods, the athlete tries to position the joints to enhance the sought flexibility. Then the performer statically maintains the position for a number of seconds for each set. The athlete then builds the time requirement progressively over a long period. Static stretching is pressure solely from the athlete's own force, and PNF is pressure applied by a partner.

Ballistic stretching involves bobbing or active movements to the limits of motion. The athlete does not hold the final position. For instance, take a standing position with arms above the head and feet apart. Lower the trunk dynamically toward the knees to reach maximum range of motion. Repeat this several times, in each repetition attempting to reach the most acute angle. Stop when you feel any discomfort or pain.

PNF involves stretching to the limits of motion, doing a static contraction for a few seconds against the resistance of a partner. The athlete then lifts the limb voluntarily to a more acute angle beyond previous limits. Once again, the athlete performs the same routine, a strong isometric contraction against the resistance of a partner.

Designing a Program

The best time to start developing flexibility is during the initiation stage, because the early stages of anatomical development in children do not play any restrictive role. During this stage, aim training programs at developing all joints, especially hips, shoulders, and ankles. Ankle flexibility is crucial for any skills requiring running and jumping, and athletes must use flexion and extension to bring the toes toward or away from the calf. I advise the static method, with maximum attention at the extreme point of the stretch where discomfort may result from overstretching. Don't overdo it!

Flexibility training should also be emphasized throughout the formation stage. This allows the child to continue developing strong joints while addressing the anatomical problems (such as the legs growing disproportionately and a change in leverage between the legs and the trunk) that may occur during puberty. The more time you dedicate to developing flexibility during prepubescence and pubescence, the fewer problems will appear in the later stages of athletic development.

A flexibility session should not be boring! You can combine it with play and games; however, do not create a competitive environment because this can result in overstretching and eventual harm.

The flexibility that athletes develop during prepubescence is general or overall flexibility. What they develop from pubescence on you can regard as specific or sport specific. As such, parents, instructors, and coaches should pay attention to the joints required in a given sport, particularly ankle and hip flexibility because these areas have been underemphasized in the past. This does not mean that you should neglect the other joints. Athletes need a maintenance program in place for the non-specific joints during puberty and throughout their athletic careers.

Orient flexibility in the specialization stage toward maximizing specific flexibility, giving it a dynamic or ballistic emphasis. Remember that athletes perform sports and certain moves ballistically. As such, the athletes have to train to perform moves dynamically and with the highest amplitude. It is the lack of such training that results in injuries and not the nature of the ballistic exercises themselves. If an athlete does not have adequate flexibility, even this mechanism might not help. Develop good flexibility to protect athletes from injury.

For the annual periodization of flexibility, athletes must strive to gain most of their flexibility during the off-season. Regard the competitive season as a maintenance period, when athletes will direct the energy and strain they place on muscle groups toward specific training. In either case, flexibility has to be part of every-day training, and athletes should incorporate flexibility exercises at the end of the warm-up part of a training lesson. Increase the range of motion of an exercise progressively and carefully throughout performances. At first, athletes may perform exercises with an amplitude, magnitude, and extension that does not challenge them; then they should increase progressively up to their limits. From this point on, each repetition should aim at reaching this maximum limit and even furthering it.

View the following exercises only as guidelines. Parents and instructors can incorporate many other exercises, as long as athletes do them in a progressive way. All the exercises in this chapter are appropriate for all stages of athletic development. Some of the exercises have ballistic and PNF options that may be used with athletes in the specialized stage of training. Please refer to tables 3.1 and 3.2 for an example of an appropriate progression.

Table 3.1	Periodization Model for Flexibility Training	
Stage of development	**Training method**	**Exercises**
Initiation	Static	• Trunk and hip flexion • Large body circles • Flex to opposite leg • Ankle double touch • Seated toe touch • Straddle stretch • Opposite toe touch
Athletic formation	Static PNF	• Hamstring stretch • Shoulder bow stretch • Ankle stretch • Diagonal ankle press • Double kicks • Exercises with a partner to enhance flexibility by using the static and PNF method, on the floor and standing.
Specialization	Static PNF Ballistic	• Perform stretching exercises with and without a partner using static and PNF methods. • You can use most exercises with partners for ballistic flexibility. For ballistic stretching, be careful at the extreme points of flexibility.

Note: Refer to exercises on the following pages.

Table 3.2	Progression for Flexibility Training			
Type of flexibility	**Stage of development**	**Number of reps or seconds per set**	**Number of sets per joint**	**Rest interval between sets**
Static	Prepuberty	4-5 sec	2	1 min
	Puberty	6-8 sec	2-3	1 min
	Postpuberty	6-12 sec	3-4	30 sec
PNF	Puberty	6-10 sec	3-4	1 min
	Postpuberty	6-12 sec	3-5	30 sec
Ballistic	Postpuberty	4-8 reps	2-4	30 sec

Note: The ballistic method is for postpuberty on, only after achieving high degrees of flexibility during prepuberty and puberty via static and PNF methods.

TRUNK AND HIP FLEXION

Area stretched: hips and side of the trunk

1. Stand with feet shoulder-width apart and arms at your sides, palms facing up.

2. Bend the body to the left swinging right arm over head until palms are touching. Keep elbows straight. Hold for four to six seconds.

3. Repeat on the right.

LARGE BODY CIRCLES

Area stretched: trunk, hips, and hamstrings

1. Stand with feet shoulder-width apart and arms above the head, palms together.

2. Make large rotations with arms and body, down the left side to the floor and up the right side to above the head.

3. Repeat four rotations in the opposite direction.

FLEX TO OPPOSITE LEG

Area stretched: hips, trunk, and hamstrings

1. Stand with feet wider than shoulder-width apart and arms above the head.

2. Flex the hips, driving the right arm toward the foot of the left leg; leave the left arm up and hold for four to six seconds.

3. Return to the starting position.

4. Repeat the movement with the other arm toward the opposite leg for four to six seconds.

5. Return to the starting position.

ANKLE DOUBLE TOUCH

Area stretched: hips, chest, shoulders, and hamstrings

1. Stand with feet apart and arms above the head.

2. Flex the upper body, touching the opposite leg with each hand, and hold for four to eight seconds.

3. Bring the upper body to the horizontal, swinging the arms to the side and up.

4. Return to the starting position.

SEATED TOE TOUCH

Area stretched: hips, hamstrings, and calves

1. Sit with legs straight and arms extended above the head.

2. Flex the upper body forward while exhaling, with arms extended as far as possible toward toes, and hold for four to six seconds.

3. Return to the starting position.

STRADDLE STRETCH

Area stretched: hips, shoulders, and calves

1. Lie on your back with arms stretched over head, and toes pointed.

2. Raise the upper body and flex it over the legs attempting to touch hands to toes. Hold for four to six seconds.

3. Return to the starting position.

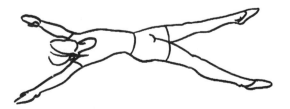

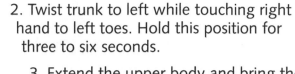

OPPOSITE TOE TOUCH

Area stretched: hips, hamstrings, and shoulders

1. Kneel on right leg, left leg extended forward, arms raised to shoulder level.

2. Twist trunk to left while touching right hand to left toes. Hold this position for three to six seconds.

3. Extend the upper body and bring the right leg back to the starting position.

4. Repeat with the opposite leg.

Variation

Perform this exercise by extending the leg diagonally.

HAMSTRING STRETCH

Area stretched: hamstrings and hips

1. Flex the knees and hips, and place your hand on the floor.

2. Extend the knees, keeping the hands on the floor, and hold for three to five seconds.

3. Return to the starting position.

STRADDLE MEDICINE BALL ROTATIONS

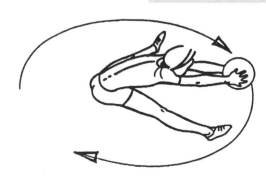

Area stretched: shoulders, groin, hips, and hamstrings

1. Sit with legs far apart, holding a medicine ball in front of the chest.

2. Perform a complete, large rotation to the right.

3. Repeat to the other side.

SHOULDER BOW STRETCH

Area stretched: shoulders and chest

1. Kneel on both legs, with hips flexed and arms on the floor above the head.

2. Press the chest toward the floor for four to six seconds.

3. Return to starting position. Repeat three to six times.

HURDLE STRETCH

Area stretched: back, hips, quadriceps, and shoulders

1. Sit with right knee bent and pointing to the side, left leg extended, and arms together above the head.

2. Flex the hips, lowering the arms attempting to touch hands to left foot. Hold for three to four seconds.

3. Raise the upper body, lowering it backward toward the floor, and hold three to four seconds.

4. Return to starting position.

5. Repeat, alternating each leg.

Note: To do this exercise ballistically, perform hip flexion dynamically, bobbing three or four times.

ANKLE STRETCH

Area stretched: calf muscles

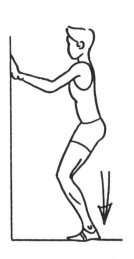

1. Stand in front of a wall with feet together and far enough away from the wall so the knees don't reach the wall. Place hands on wall at chest level.

2. Bend ankles and knees toward the wall, and hold for six to eight seconds without lifting the heels off the floor. The main pressure should be on both ankles.

3. Return to starting position.

Note: To perform this exercise ballistically, move the knees up and down ballistically six to eight times.

DIAGONAL ANKLE PRESS

Area stretched: calf muscles

1. Stand in front of a wall with feet together. Place hands on the wall at chest level. Move feet as far away from the wall as possible.

2. Bend the knees slightly, forcing the ankles to bend as much as possible without lifting the heels off the floor, and hold for six to ten seconds.

3. Return to the starting position.

Note: For ballistic stretch, raise heels off the floor and bob them back dynamically.

SEA LION STRETCH

Area stretched: trunk and groin

1. Lay on stomach, flexing arms and placing hands on the ground at shoulder level.

2. Extend the arms, arching the upper body while the hips are still on the ground. Hold this position for two to four seconds.

3. Flex the arms and lower the upper body to the starting position.

DOUBLE KICK

Area stretched: shoulders, back, and groin

1. Kneel with the hands on the floor.

2. Dynamically swing the right leg and left arm upward, arching the back.

3. Return to the starting position.

4. Repeat movement with the opposite limbs.

5. Return to starting position.

SEATED HIP FLEXION

Area stretched: hips and hamstring muscles

1. Partner A sits on the floor with arms extended. Partner B stands behind A and places hands on back.

2. Partner B presses A's upper body forward and down, holding the position for four to six seconds.

3. Relax and return to starting position.

Note: To perform it ballistically, press the trunk dynamically six to eight times.

STANDING SHOULDER STRETCH

Area stretched: chest and shoulder muscles

1. Partner A stands with arms above the head. Partner B stands behind, placing right hand below shoulder level, while left hand grasps the partner's hands.

2. Partner B presses the upper back forward and pulls the arms to extend backward. Hold the position for four to six seconds.

3. Relax and return to starting position. Alternate roles continuously.

Note: For ballistic flexibility, pull the arm dynamically backward four to eight times.

PARTNER SHOULDER STRETCH

Area stretched: chest, shoulders, groin, and abdominal muscles

1. Partner A lies on the stomach with arms above the head. Partner B stands with legs straddling A's upper body and grasps the hands.

2. Partner B slowly raises A's arms and holds the position for four seconds.

3. Return to starting position.

4. Repeat with partners changing roles.

SCALE STRETCH

Area stretched: groin, quadriceps, and trunk

1. Partner A stands three feet in front of partner B.

2. Partner A raises the left leg back and up, with upper body vertical. Partner B catches the ankle with both hands.

3. Partner B slowly presses A's leg upward. Hold in this position for two to six seconds.

4. Lower the leg and return to starting position. Alternate leg action and partners' roles.

Note: For a ballistic stretch, bob the leg upward three to six times.

Variation

While in the hold position, flex and extend the knee of the supporting leg.

PARTNER HAMSTRING STRETCH

Area stretched: hamstring and hip muscles

1. Partner A lies on the back with arms above the head. Partner B stands at A's left side.

2. Partner A raises the right leg. Partner B catches the ankle with both hands.

3. Partner B applies a constant pressure downward against the partner's leg.

4. Partner A returns the leg to the starting position.

5. Alternate legs and partners' roles.

Note: For a ballistic stretch, bob the leg downward four to eight times.

Variation

Partner A pulls the leg above the head, while partner B holds the opposite leg against the ground.

4

Motor Skills Training

Coordination is a complex motor skill necessary for high performance. Strength, speed, flexibility, and endurance represent the fitness foundation of high performance, and good coordination is necessary for skill acquisition and perfection. A well-coordinated child will always acquire a skill quickly and be able to perform it smoothly. Compared with a child who might perform a movement with stiffness and difficulty, a well-coordinated young athlete will spend less energy for the same performance. Therefore, good coordination results in more skill effectiveness.

Agility refers to athletes' ability to quickly and smoothly change directions, move with ease in the field, or fake actions to deceive their direct opponent. Balance represents the ability of an athlete to maintain and control a body position or steadiness while performing an athletic skill. This is vital, not only in gymnastics but also in most team sports, in which the balance of the body and limbs are so important in deceiving an opponent or avoiding being deceived by fake actions in the field.

Although these motor skills are largely genetically determined, they are highly trainable as well. I have designed the games and exercises in this chapter to help young athletes improve coordination, agility, and balance. By repetitively performing these skills, over time you will notice better accuracy, timing, and precision. You will also notice improvement in overall performance.

The time to train coordination is during the early years when athletes learn everything quickly. Through a well-designed multilateral program in the initiation and athletic formation stages, young athletes improve their coordination, balance, and agility. Contrary to performing just the skills of the chosen sport or just specificity training, a multi-skill program will create a solid foundation, which will enrich skills and abilities later in one's athletic career, leading to superior performance.

Recognizing the close relationships between strength, speed, and endurance as well as coordination and agility allows both instructor and athlete to understand the multilateral process. The higher the levels of strength, speed, and endurance, the easier the development of coordination and agility. For example, strength improvement helps athletes to quickly move limbs and change directions. Leg strength, or the ability to powerfully apply force against the ground, will increase speed. Achieving a good strength level will also help the young athletes to learn skills in sports, such as gymnastics, baseball, and skiing. For example, to mount a gymnastics apparatus or to learn a skill in which you lift the whole body is impossible without improving strength. Athletes will also learn batting, pitching, and throwing faster if their strength is greater. Most team sport athletes will greatly benefit from improved strength, coordination, and agility.

Irregardless of the level of inherited coordination, you cannot expect consistent gains in this important ability without giving special attention to improvement throughout childhood and adolescence. Multilateral development, the exposure to a variety of skills and exercises, will result in visible coordination gains. The higher the coordination level, the easier it is to learn new and complicated technical and tactical skills. As a result, an athlete will quickly and efficiently adjust to the unusual circumstances of athletic competition.

Although high coordination and agility are advantageous in many sports, they are most important in complex sports, such as team sports. Consequently, team sport athletes should be most concerned about performing the exercises in this chapter. All these exercises will help the young athletes to improve hand-eye coordination and smooth actions between legs and arms.

Considerations for Initiation

Prepuberty represents the most important phase in developing coordination. This is why it is called the rapid gain phase. This occurs irrespective of whether a child participates in organized and supervised sports activities or simply plays with peers.

At this development stage, children who are involved in a variety of activities make greater gains in coordination compared with those who participate in one sport that applies only sport-specific training. Multilateral training that exposes children to numerous skills, drills, games, relays, and other exercises enriches their skill experience and, as a result, improves their coordination dramatically.

During prepubescence, children develop basic skills and movements through play and games. As they participate in various physical activities, they also develop the ability to distinguish between simple and complex skills and exercises. For instance, prepuberty children will learn to dribble a basketball with their better hand. As they grow and become more comfortable with this skill, they'll also learn to dribble with the opposite hand. The next step in highly coordinated and agile dribbling will be to do that between legs, with both left and right hand. As skill improves, the player will also learn how to defend against a highly coordinated opponent or how to get the ball from someone whose skills might not be as good as his or her own.

Athletes also improve other elements of coordination during prepubescence, such as developing the feel and perception for an activity, thus enhancing their learning potential. Similar gains are visible in developing rhythm—reproducing a series of movements with regularity and pacing—as in dance and artistic sports.

Visible improvements occur in timing, or the ability to time reactions to the moves of a partner or player from the opposition. These actions also benefit from improvement in visual orientation to the surrounding environment, allowing the athlete to sense the actions and maneuvers of teammates and opposition.

Considerations for Athletic Formation

The fast coordination improvement during prepubescence sometimes slows or even slightly regresses during pubescence. Growth spurts up to 10 to 12 centimeters or 4 to 5 inches per year, specific to this stage of children's development, normally occur with disturbances in coordination. This is mostly because limb growth, especially in the legs, changes the proportions between body parts, their leverage, and, consequently, the ability to coordinate their actions proficiently.

Although these trends are evident in all children, those who practice sports continue to gain in the quality of coordination compared with other children. During pubescence these children continue to improve their balance and their

accuracy and timing of physical actions. Girls tend to improve visual orientation and rhythm of motions better than boys because of gender differences and a more natural talent for dance and artistic sports.

Differences in coordination abilities are also visible between early and late maturing children. Early maturers go through a slight coordination crises, which may temporarily affect a fine coordination of physical actions (Sharma and Hirtz, 1991). Consequently, because of their fast rhythm of physical growth, early maturers need more exercises for coordination improvement than late maturers.

Considerations for Specialization

As children approach adolescence, coordination does not develop at the same rate as during prepuberty. Following the growth spurts of puberty, children's ability to synchronize movements slightly improves culminating with postpuberty where improvement in coordination is constant. As we may expect, athletes fare much better than nonathletes, who often look awkward if they perform unfamiliar moves.

Despite concentration on sport-specific training at this stage, a variety of skills, training time for multilateral activities, and attention to continuing coordination development should remain a concern for postpubescent athletes. To ignore this and focus only on specific training may stop the improvements in coordination that are crucial for perfecting the skills for the selected sport. That's why it's important to maintain the 20-percent multilateral training discussed in chapter 1.

Designing a Program

The main objective of coordination training is to be able to perform increasingly complex skills and exercises, and to improve skill acquisition. Parents and instructors should expose young athletes to the basic skills of sprinting, jumping, throwing, catching, balancing, climbing, gymnastics, and swimming. As athletes acquire these skills, they can improve coordination by extending the complexity of skills and exercises and by enhancing the difficulty of performing them. At the same time, teach the athletes new skills from the selected sport or other sports, progressively demanding higher quality performance. As mentioned earlier, coordination proficiency and learning ability may plateau if the athletes do not constantly challenge themselves but rather perform the same skill all the time.

I express the training program for coordination in simpler form than the other training programs in this book. Because it is difficult to measure, there are no specific training methods for measuring the load or number of sets and repetitions for coordination.

Table 4.1 suggests a long-term, comprehensive periodization model for coordination, agility, balance, and skills. Exercises become more challenging as the athlete progresses through each development stage. During the initiation and athletic formation stages, the coach tries to develop the main elements of coordination. This will eventually lead the athletes to a sport-specific form of training in later stages with complex, performance-oriented activities. The model does not pretend to exhaust all the possibilities. Please use it as a guideline that enriches your experience and expertise.

Exposing children to coordination exercises in the early years (prepuberty) of athletic development is essential to skill acquisition. Good coordination will make a child learn a skill faster which will translate into better performance in their late teens. This is why it is crucial during prepuberty and puberty to include exercises for developing coordination, balance, spatial orientation, and body awareness (such as those in table 4.1) in every physical activity. Because many of the suggested exercises are simple, coaches, teachers, or parents can incorporate

Table 4.1	Periodization Model for Motor Skills Training	
Stage of development	**Forms of training**	**Exercises**
Initiation	Preparatory exercises for skill acquisition	• Rolling • Kicking • Throwing • Dribbling • Catching
	Simple balance	• Walking on narrow lines • Jumping on/off low objects
	Simple rhythm and reaction time	• Catching
	Simple spatial orientation and sense of body/limb position	• Crawling/rolling • Front somersault • Throwing • Catching
	Simple hand-eye coordination	• Dribbling • Throwing • Catching
	Skill-enhancing exercises	• Ball exercises • Ball exercises with partner • Ball hits and throws • Catching skills • Rebounding ball catch • Dribbling • Relays
	Advanced balance exercises	• Scissors-kick handstand • Backward roll • Cartwheel • Cartwheel against the wall

(continued)

Table 4.1	(continued)	
Stage of development	**Forms of Training**	**Exercises**
Athletic formation	Advanced hand-eye coordination	• Ball throws and catches • Ball hits • Rebounding ball catches
	Limbs coordination	• Coordination for limbs • Skipping rope • Ball throws and catches
	Advanced spatial orientation	• Skipping rope • Backward roll • Scissors-kick handstand • Cartwheel
	Signal analysis and reaction to various stimuli	• Handstands • Ball exercises with partner • Games • Relays
	Advanced hand-eye coordination	• Jumps with turns and ball throws • Games • Relays
Specialization	Skill perfection	• Rolls and rotations • Ball throws and catch games • Relays
	Complex spatial orientation	• Jumps with turns • Games • Jumps over objects • Rolls and jumps
	Balance and body control/body awareness	• Rolls and turns • Jumps over objects and turns • All variations of body balance • Games • Relays
	Improve anticipation	• Rolls and turns • Throws and catches with partner • Balance exercises • Games

Table 4.1 *(continued)*

Stage of development	Forms of Training	Exercises
Specialization	Analysis-reorientation	• Rolls and turns of 180-360 degrees • Rolls, ball throws, and catches • Games • Relays

Note: Refer to exercises at the end of this chapter.

them in any formal training session they organize in a backyard, basement, or playground.

All age groups should do 10 to 15 minutes of coordination, agility, and balance work at every workout. It should be done in the early part of a training session immediately after a warm-up because children learn best when they are fresh. Table 4.2 shows an example of a typical workout for the initiation phase. (As children improve coordination or grow older, increase the difficulty of coordination and balance exercises.)

Some I suggest for initiation or athletic formation could be used for specialization as well. Select exercises according to the individual's abilities and athletic potential. For the more difficult exercises such as a somersault, cartwheel, or jumps, children need assistance and support from a parent or instructor to avoid discomfort or injury.

It is important to constantly observe a good progression such as the following:

• Simple exercises should lead to more complex ones (i.e., learn target kick first, then foot dribble).

• Known exercises should lead to unknown ones (i.e., from cartwheel to handstand).

Table 4.2 Sample Workout for Prepuberty

Part	Scope	Forms of Training	Duration
1	Warm-up	• Jogging, stretching	5 min
2	Coordination/balance	• Preparation for skill acquisition • Hand-eye coordination • Spatial orientation • Simple balance	10-15 min
3	Play, game	• Skill acquisition from the chosen sport	20-30 min
4	Cool-down	• 2-3 relays • Easy stretching	5 min

Note: Use table 4.1 for examples of exercises for each form of training.

Exercises and Skills

To make this book practical for all users, I suggest several exercises. Please note that athletes can perform most exercises at home. Others they must perform in a gym or fitness club. An adult should always supervise children. These exercises do not exhaust all that are available in the field; however, they will develop coordination in the basic skills of jumping, batting, dribbling, kicking a ball, and so on, using a variety of apparatuses such as utility balls (a basic rubber ball children play with), to baseballs, and medicine balls. Medicine balls received their name from the field of medicine, where they were used in therapeutic medicine and rehabilitation for over 100 years. The best medicine balls are made of rubber. They are available in different sizes and weigh between 3 and 14 pounds (2 and 6 kilograms).

FRONT SOMERSAULT

Focus: coordination, agility, body awareness

1. Squat, arms extended to front.

2. Place hands on the floor, tuck the head, bend elbows, and slowly extend the knees for a forward front roll, keeping the back round.

3. After the roll is complete, bend the knees to end up in a squatting position.

UTILITY BALL DRIBBLING

Focus: hand-eye coordination, timing

1. Begin standing, kneeling, or sitting.

2. Perform at first two-hand, then one-hand dribbling.

Variation

• Dribble the ball back and forth with a partner.

TARGET KICK

Focus: coordination, awareness (distance, direction), passing and kicking accuracy

1. Begin standing.

2. Kick the ball, with each leg alternately, toward the target (i.e., another ball, cone, etc.).

FOOT DRIBBLE

Focus: leg-eye coordination

1. Stand with the ball on the ground in front of one leg.

2. Dribble the ball forward, sideways, with both feet, and with both sides of the foot.

COORDINATION FOR LIMBS

Focus: limb coordination

1. Stand with arms at the sides.

2. Circle both arms forward.

3. Circle both arms backward.

Variations

• Circle one arm at a time in both directions.

• Circle left arm forward and right arm backward at the same time.

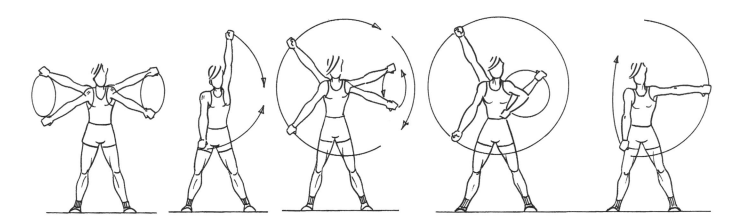

SKIPPING ROPE

Focus: limb coordination

1. Stand holding one end of the rope in each hand.

2. Do continuous jumping.

Variations

• High tuck jumps.

• Jump on one foot, repeat using other foot.

• Straight jumps, crossing the arms.

BACKWARD ROLL

Focus: limb coordination, spatial orientation

1. Crouch, grabbing the knees with both hands.

2. Roll backward on the back, palms ready to be placed on the floor below the shoulders.

3. Straighten the legs, touch the toes, then push with the arms to complete a backward roll into a squat position.

SCISSORS-KICK HANDSTAND

Focus: balance, spatial orientation

1. Stand with arms above the head and one leg extended in front.

2. Step forward, placing hands on mat or carpet. Keep arms straight; kick one leg up, then the other leg. Bring the first leg down, then the second leg, to standing position.

CARTWHEEL

Focus: balance, spatial orientation

1. Draw a line on the ground. Stand with feet apart.

2. Step sideways, lowering arms to the floor, and kick legs vertically over the hands (straight).

3. Bring the first leg down along the line, then the second leg, back to the side-standing position with legs apart.

Variation

Cartwheel against the wall, then cartwheel down.

BEHIND OVERHEAD THROW

Focus: skill, hand-eye coordination

1. Stand with feet apart holding the ball behind the seat.

2. Flex the body and throw the ball up and forward.

3. Extend the body and catch the ball above the head.

BETWEEN-LEG THROW

Focus: skill enhancement, hand-eye coordination

1. Partners stand facing each other.

2. Partner A bounces the ball between the legs to partner B.

3. Partner B catches the ball and repeats the action.

OVERHAND SIMULTANEOUS THROW

Focus: hand-eye coordination

1. Partners stand two to four feet apart, facing each other. Each partner is holding a ball in one hand.

2. Each partner simultaneously bounces the ball to the other partner.

3. Each partner catches the ball in the opposite hand.

4. Repeat the movement, bouncing the ball from the hand that caught the ball.

REBOUNDING BALL CATCH

Focus: hand-eye coordination, throwing and catching accuracy

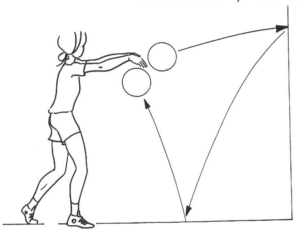

1. Stand in front of a wall or wooden fence.

2. Throw the ball against the wall, let it rebound off the ground, and catch it.

Variations

• Throw the ball against the ground.

• Rebound toward the wall then toward the player who catches it.

• Throw the ball against the wall and catch it.

• Do the same with one hand.

TWO-HAND CHEST AND OVERHEAD PASS

Focus: hand-eye coordination, passing and catching accuracy

1. Two rows of players face inward at 10 to 15 feet (3-5meters) apart, one player at the end of a row holding a ball.

2. Throw the ball against the ground, rebounding toward an opposite player. The player catches the ball, repeating the same toward another player.

Variation

• Do the same with one hand, alternating hands.

OVERHAND ZIGZAG AND TARGET THROW

Focus: hand-eye coordination, throwing accuracy

1. Two rows of players stand 10 to 15 feet (3-5meters) apart, one player holding a tennis, baseball, or any other type of ball.

2. Overhand throw toward a player or at a target.

3. Alternate hands.

OVERHAND THROW RELAY

Focus: hand-eye coordination, passing accuracy

1. Divide the group into two teams. Players line up one behind the other. One team member stands opposite the team.

2. Throw the ball to the first team member, who catches it and throws it back.

3. After throwing the ball back to the person in front, the thrower sits down.

4. This continues until the whole team sits. The team who finishes first is the winner.

Note: Change the teams to be as equal in skills as possible.

ROLLING TARGET

Focus: hand-eye coordination, skill, throwing accuracy

1. Divide the class into small teams. One at a time, the teams take turns throwing rubber balls at a medicine ball that is rolled across the gym floor. The students must stand behind a designated line.

2. Record each team's score (number of hits).

3. Use both left and right arms.

OVER THE NET GAME (VOLLEYBALL COURT)

Focus: hand-eye coordination, throwing and catching accuracy

1. Using a utility ball or medicine ball, the goal is to toss the ball over the net and have it land on the floor.

2. Using the principles of volleyball, players may pass the ball to teammates up to two times before they must throw it back over the net.

DODGE GAME

Focus: hand-eye coordination, throwing accuracy

1. Two teams start at their home wall. Place three balls in the center of the gym.

2. At the start there is a dash for the balls, and the players who get them first must throw from their side to hit members of the other team.

3. If hit, a player must go along the side of the gym to the opposite wall.

4. While at the other wall, if an errant ball comes within reach, he or she may use it to hit the opposing player despite being captured. Hit only below the waist.

5. The game ends when one team is entirely captured.

V-SIT BALANCE

Focus: balance

1. Sit, palms on the floor at the sides of the body.

2. Raise arms to horizontal and extend legs up in front of the body.

3. Maintain the balance in this position.

4. Return to starting position.

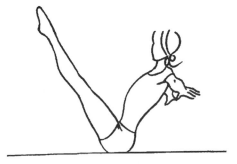

HANDSTAND

Focus: balance, skill

1. The instructor stands facing the athlete.

2. The athlete takes a short step forward, extending arms toward ground.

3. Kick one leg upward toward the instructor, who catches the athlete by the hips.

4. Bring the other leg forward into the handstand.

5. Return to the starting position.

BACKROLL INTO A HANDSTAND

Focus: balance, skill

1. Back roll on hips, back into a handstand. Lower one leg, then the other into standing position.

ROLLS WITH TURNS

Focus: balance, spatial orientation

1. From a standing position, front roll jump half turn to back roll jump half turn (180 degrees).

Variations

• Continuously repeat movement.

• Perform the movement with a full 360-degree turn.

JUMP AND ROLL WITH TURN

Focus: spatial orientation, body control

1. Stand to one side of a horizontally suspended rope or ribbon.

2. Jump over the rope into an immediate front roll with a half turn (180 degrees).

3. Perform in the opposite direction.

Variation

Continuously repeat the movement. (i.e., jump over the rope, front roll, jump, half turn).

THROW, ROLL, AND CATCH

Focus: spatial orientation, body awareness

1. Begin standing.

2. Throw the ball up and forward.

3. Perform a front roll.

4. Catch the ball.

WALK THE PLANK

Focus: balance, body control

1. Stand at the end of a two-by-four plank.

2. Walk forward, sideways, and backward without falling off the plank.

Variations

• Do the same with the arms performing circles, forward and backward.

• Do crossover steps in both directions.

• Raise bent or straight leg with arms to the side.

• Do forward and backward walks over several utility balls placed 2 feet (60 centimeters) apart.

• Hold a scale for three to six seconds.

• Walk on toes.

• Do turns of 180 degrees on the toes.

• Do the same with a 360-degree rotation.

• Do forward walking with a slight leap at the end of the plank.

chapter 5

Speed Training

Speed is important for most sports, because the majority of athletes must either run, move, react, or change direction quickly. The term speed incorporates three elements, including reaction time (the motor reaction to a signal), movement time (the ability to move a limb quickly, as in martial arts, batting, or passing a ball), and speed of running (including the frequency of arm and leg movement).

In team sports an athlete rarely performs a straight line action, such as sprinting in track and field. Players are highly regarded if they can quickly change directions to receive a pass or to deceive an opponent. In either case, elements of speed are combined: here, they are reaction time and speed of running in different directions. Additionally, take for instance a quick arm or leg action in martial arts, in which an athlete is either delivering a fast blow or quickly reacting, and as a result blocking or avoiding a fast blow. In either case, such an athlete has to be fast, or have a fast movement time. This is why it is important to understand, and to train, the different elements of speed.

Each sport has its type of specific speed and quickness training. However, parents and coaches can help their young athletes by performing additional speed work. The examples at the end of this chapter will assist in your quest for speed gains.

Many sports specialists believe that sprinters are born, not made, because speed is largely genetically determined, depending on the athlete's muscle-type composition. The higher the proportion of fast-twitch to slow-twitch muscle fibers, the faster the reaction and more powerful the muscle contraction. Although speed is associated with genetics, genetics are not the limit. There are ways to develop speed through training. Even athletes who do not have a natural talent in speed-related activities can significantly improve their speed. It is important for future athletes to emphasize speed training during childhood. Running speed, reaction time, and quick footwork improve continuously from five years of age to maturity.

Speed improvement also depends on the ability of muscles to contract forcefully, so the body or a limb moves fast. Therefore, a forceful contraction in any type of quickness or speed relates to strength training. Because children's strength is visible mainly from puberty on, they achieve most gains in speed during puberty and postpuberty. However, speed improvements are visible also during prepuberty, as a result of neural adaptation, meaning that as children perform quickness and speed activities, the muscles learn to work together and become more effective. Therefore, speed gains during prepuberty are not the result of powerful muscle contractions but the outcome of neuromuscular adaptation.

Speed Training Model for Initiation

The ability of prepubescent children to perform quick motions increases progressively in this early stage with both boys and girls developing speed in the later stage. Most speed gains come not only from learning the sprinting skills, but also from developing a better muscle coordination.

Some children, especially those who do not experience multilateral development, may have poor arm and leg coordination. Because arm drive directly influences the leg frequency, a low level of coordinating arm and shoulder force impedes the ability of children to run fast.

Gender differences in running speed are not visible during early prepubescence. This starts to show as children approach puberty, with the trend being that boys perform speed-related activities better than girls. Other forms of speed and agility display the same tendency (Bailey, Malina, and Mirwald 1985; Hebbelinck 1989).

Scope of Speed Training

One main goal of prepubescent sport activities is to develop a play-specific speed. Through exposure to play, games, and relays, children will learn how to coordinate their arms and legs, make them move faster, and run on the balls of the feet. Children's movement time will improve as a result of such motor experiences. They will learn how quickly to start moving parts of the body at a signal or in a play situation.

Prepubescent speed development is mainly the result of nervous system adaptation children achieve through play and games. As a result of this motor experience, the nervous system learns how to coordinate the actions of the arms and legs most effectively. Consequently, a child will progressively cover a certain distance, change directions, and react more quickly.

Children enjoy knowing that they are fast. They have fun and like performing physical tasks in which speed is important, both during play and relays. Variety, in speed exercises is important because it improves motor experience. At the same time, children should not neglect the upper body. Simple throws using a tennis ball or light medicine ball are useful for developing upper-body movement time.

As children improve their limb coordination, they can progressively participate in simple speed drills, especially as they approach puberty. Similarly, for those involved in organized training, like team sports, the instructor can perform specific drills for speed, in most cases using a ball. The instructor can organize sport-specific drills as part of training, and children can perform other types of speed training in addition to the technical work (see the exercises at the end of this chapter).

Unless children participate in gender-specific teams, most games, plays, and relays, especially in the school curriculum, should be coed, because at this development stage there are no visible differences between boys and girls (Bailey, Malina, and Mirwald 1985).

Program Design

You should view any speed training program for prepubescence as an early nervous system adaptation to a variety of movements. As the nervous coordination of the muscles improves, so will the children's capacity to be faster.

The duration of a drill or the distance to run should not be long. Children should not experience discomfort at this age. They should not run fast and continuously for longer than four to six seconds, because longer distances require specific training. If they pause for two or three minutes, then they could repeat the same action with enjoyment. There is no fun when there is discomfort and pain.

Instructors should plan training programs for speed, like anything else, over several years. The instructor should use a variety of exercises that involve the whole body and stimulate running speed and movement time for both arms and legs. Play, games, and relays should be the major elements to improve speed for prepuberty.

Athletes should increase distance progressively over years, from 20 meters or yards to 40 to 50 meters or yards, especially for children who are approaching puberty. Children should perform primary running exercises in a straight line. As children approach puberty and become stronger, you can incorporate running in zigzag, stop and go, slalom, and with quick turns in training. Stop and go is a speed drill in which the athletes run as fast as possible for 5 to 15 meters or yards, and at the signal "stop," they stop running as quickly as possible. At the signal "go," they run as fast as possible in another direction, which the instructor points out, for a further 5 to 15 meters or yards.

To improve upper-body movement time, I advise throwing tennis balls, medicine balls, and baseballs. Also, relays using medicine balls for throwing and carrying will benefit upper-body strength, which will later positively influence movement time. For further information on these exercises, please see chapter 6, "Strength and Power Training".

In team sport training, or during games, the instructor can combine speed tasks with skill performance such as throwing and kicking the ball. Such drills are typical combinations for developing running speed and movement time. Prepubescent children have good trainability for speed, especially as they approach puberty; however, you should carefully plan and progressively implement everything.

Table 5.1 incorporates several elements of speed training useful in most sports. Under the column "Forms of training" are the types of activities children can perform; "Duration or distance of activity" suggests how many minutes, meters, or yards to run. The next column suggests how many times to repeat an activity. Finally, between repetitions, children need to rest, relax, and avoid an undesirable stress for this age.

For prepuberty, the duration of a game does not have to be longer than 20 or 30 minutes. In hockey or soccer, children can play the game for two periods. I do not advise prepubescent children to play a game for the same duration as adult athletes, because at this age children do not have the conditioning potential to play a 90-minute soccer game or three 20-minute hockey games. An exhausted child hardly thinks about the next game, whereas one who has been tired but enjoyed it is eagerly waiting for the next game.

Children can easily repeat relays performed over 10 to 15 meters or yards three to five times, especially if they use different relays. However, irrespective of how eager children may be to repeat it, make sure they have a rest interval between relays to rest and relax.

For team sports, speed training has to take the form of running with turns, direction changes, and stop and go. Because the distance for this type of work is not long, children can perform more repetitions (four to eight) with a two- or three-minute rest interval between them. The structure of a workout for speed training may follow the example of table 5.2.

Speed Training Model for Athletic Formation

Speed development increases during puberty. Most children experience an acceleration in speed development during this stage, a phenomenon that is valid for

Table 5.1   Periodization Model for Speed Training for Prepuberty

Forms of training	Duration or distance of activity	Number of reps	Rest interval (min)
Games	20-30 min	1-2	—
Relays	10-15 m/(10-15)yd	3-5	2-3
Speed training	10-50 m/(10-15)yd	4-6	3-4
Speed training with turns, changes of direction, and stop and go	5-15 m/(10-15)yd	4-8	2-3

Table 5.2   Speed Training Session

Part	Objective	Exercises	Duration or number of reps
1	Warm-up	Same as table 4.1 (pg. 47)	10 min
2	Improve speed		6 × 25 sec
	Improve game-specific speed	• Short and fast technical/tactical drills with quick direction changes	8 × 15 sec
		• Play/game/scrimmage with technical/tactical goals	20-30 min
3	Cool-down, relaxation, enjoyment	• Relays	3 reps
		• Relaxed, easy jogging	3 min

both boys and girls. Such improvement may relate to increase in body and muscle size.

Strength gains positively influence speed development. From puberty on, the testosterone level in boys starts to increase dramatically, along with the ability to increase strength. The direct result of strength gains is improving speed, both running speed and movement time.

Although boys show clear improvements from the later stages of pubescence, girls seem to plateau in their rate of speed development. Some speed gains can result from improved nervous system coordination of the muscles involved in quick actions. Most of it, however, is the consequence of strength development and the ability of the muscles to contract more powerfully. As a result, the arms can drive more forcefully and the legs can push with more power against the ground.

Gains in upper-body power, especially the arms, improve movement time, reflecting the ability to throw the ball farther or to bat more powerfully. On the other hand, improved leg strength translates into kicking the ball with more power. For most team sports in which running speed is important, the ability to quickly change directions is also significant. This skill is the result of improved nervous system coordination and strength gain of the muscles involved.

Scope of Speed Training

Speed training during puberty has to become specific to improve it to higher levels. However, it should still be part of a multilateral athletic development, and children should do it in connection with developing other abilities.

During puberty, quickness and high acceleration training lead to a better nervous system adaptation, which results in enhanced coordination of muscles performing the arm and leg actions. As strength starts to improve, especially for boys, movement time increases, which influences upper-body quickness and running speed. Similarly, as leg strength improves, children start to push more forcefully against the ground and are able to drive their bodies forward much faster.

Although coed speed training may occur during prepubescence, I advise that you separate the genders starting from pubescence. As mentioned, from puberty on, boys become stronger, which positively influences the rate of limb movement and speed. As a result of these differences, it is better for girls and boys to train in separate groups.

Program Design

As children approach postpubescence, they can increase the total amount of speed training. Whether using exercises such as play, games, relays, or even sprinting routines, they can progressively increase the distance run with high velocity from 20 to 50 or 60 meters or yards.

Speed training can be fun for children and instructors alike. You can perform a variety of exercises involving play, games, and especially relays. You can organize relays in ways that use many exercises, such as sprints, sprints with turns, runs around cones with direction changes, carrying or throwing medicine balls, or jumps over safe equipment at a low height.

You ought to organize special exercises to improve reaction time as well. The intention is to decrease the time it takes for the child to move a limb, for instance, the arms and legs in running or the arms in throwing a ball. You can achieve such a goal in two simple phases:

1. During the early part of improving movement time, the instructor positions him or herself in front of the children, facing them. At his or her signal, visual (clap) or sound (whistle), the children perform the task. Because children can see the instructor, they can start the action faster.

2. As children improve their reaction time, after a few months or one to two years, the instructor will select a position behind the children so he or she can see the children but cannot be seen. Now the children will rely on sound only. The purpose of this exercise is the same; at the signal the children perform the task as quickly as possible.

Parallel with speed and movement time exercises, children should participate in simple exercises for power improvement. For the upper body, they can use a

Teaching Correct Running Technique

To improve running efficiency, athletes should work on running form technique. A crucial component in achieving such a goal is good arm drive. Arms are driven back, forward, and up to the face level. The leg frequency increases as the rate of the arm drive increases, because the rate of leg movement is led and coordinated by arm drive and frequency. The thigh of the driving leg (for our example, this will be the right leg) should reach a horizontal line; from this point on the foot of the same leg is projected forward and down. The back of the foot lands on the ground through a brushing action. As the body moves forward, the other (left) leg is driven forward. The right leg is now pushing against the ground, projecting the body forward. These actions are repeated for as long as the sprints last.

As children perform these exercises, the instructor or teacher should constantly observe them for good form, keeping shoulders down and relaxed, driving the arms simultaneously, and bringing the knees high. The position of the body is vertical, with the eyes focused ahead. The foot strikes the ground quickly, coming underneath the body as it moves forward. The running step has the following phases:

1. The propulsion phase, pushing against the ground with power to drive the body quickly forward.

2. The drive phase, in which the opposite leg drives forward, with the thigh horizontal. The opposite arm also drives along the body, with the hand at shoulder height (arms are bent at 90 degrees). It is essential to keep the ankle locked up to the landing phase.

3. Landing phase, as the foot strikes the ground, it quickly comes underneath the body.

4. Recovery phase, when the heel of the propelling leg quickly drives toward the buttock while the opposite arm quickly moves forward.

variety of medicine ball throws. Similarly, tennis and baseball throws for distance, alternating the arms for balance development, are fun and beneficial for upper-body power development. Children can develop leg power by performing simple jumps on, off, and over low and safe equipment. (Please refer to chapter 6, Strength and Power Training)

As postpubescence approaches, children can progressively increase to the maximum intensity (speed) and power of exercises to improve neuromuscular coordination. They can follow the same trend for the number of repetitions. As children show better adaptation to training, they can increase the number of repetitions, depending on their work tolerance capacity.

A critical element in speed training is the duration of the rest interval between repetitions. Because the ability to repeat high-quality exercises depends on the freshness of the neuromuscular system, the rest interval between repetitions must be as long as necessary to achieve almost full recovery and restoration of the fuel needed to produce energy.

As table 5.3 illustrates, you can use relays for developing speed for pubescence, but of longer distance than for prepuberty: 10 to 30 meters or yards, repeated four to six times, with a rest interval of two or three minutes. Children can repeat speed training in a straight line of 20 to 50 meters or yards five to eight times with a longer rest interval, four or five minutes, between each repetition. During the rest, stretch the muscles for a better relaxation. For team sports, children can perform speed training with changes of direction, turns, and stop and go for 5 to 25 meters or yards, repeated 5 to 10 times, with a rest between them of two or three minutes. Game-specific skills performed fast also develop specific speed.

If in a training session children repeat just speed training, or speed with turns and direction changes, the number of repetitions can be much higher, after which the coach will do either technical and tactical drills, play games, or scrimmage.

The structure of a training session for pubescent children can be the same as table 5.2, with the difference that duration and the number of repetitions will follow table 5.3.

Speed-Training Model for Specialization

Speed improvement comes with age. As children enter the postpuberty stage, gains in speed and movement time are more visible, especially for boys. Girls show the highest speed gains during late puberty and early postpuberty. From this point on, they seem to reach a plateau that may last throughout postpuberty unless they implement a speed-training program.

Boys maintain speed development throughout postpuberty. As they become stronger, they also become faster. Probably the biggest difference between boys and girls is in the area of upper-body strength, because from puberty on the upper-body strength gains of boys are constantly increasing.

For children involved in sports, speed gains may also relate to improved muscle coordination. As a result of multilateral training, they learn how to use their muscles and how to coordinate them for the best efficiency. As such, speed improvement also comes from better muscle and limb coordination. In addition,

Table 5.3	**Periodization Model for Speed Training for Puberty**		
Forms of training	Distance of activity	Number of reps and sets	Rest interval (min)
Relays	10-30 m/yd	4-6	2-3
Speed training (including starts)	20-50 m/yd	5-8	4-5
Speed training with turns, changes of direction, stop and go	5-25 m/yd	5-10	2-3

the nervous system learns to be more selective in choosing how fast and in what manner to react to an athletic situation. As a result of processing the signal or a game situation, the nervous system selects the action and stimulates the necessary muscles to contract and perform the quick movement.

Scope of Speed Training

Postpubescence speed training should become specific and relate to the needs of the selected sport. Reduce the play and game approach to leave time for sport-specific speed training.

For any athlete who intends to climb the ladder of high performance, postpubescence is the key link. On the one hand, anything the athletes missed during the first two stages of development, they can still correct. On the other, failing to address the sport-specific needs of speed training during prepubescence can drastically impair athletes' chances of reaching high performance. Although speed training becomes progressively more sport specific according to the athletes' needs, they should not totally dismiss fun and elements of multilateral training.

Most speed training has to be dynamic and performed with high intensity to constantly stimulate the neuromuscular system. This type of training will result in running with higher leg frequency and velocity.

A constant concern in speed training is for the athlete to learn to relax his or her antagonistic muscles as the agonistic muscles contract to perform the movements. Allot special time for training lessons in which athletes learn how to relax and perform smooth, easy, flowing, and well-coordinated skills or movements. This is possible by first performing repetitions of speed work with lower velocity, so the athlete can concentrate on relaxing the antagonistic muscles. As they achieve this, they can progressively increase the velocity until they can do the same repetition with maximum velocity. However, athletes will not achieve this training goal in a day, a week, or even a month. Sometimes it may take one or two years. Considering the benefits of learning to run smoothly, relax, and perform flowing actions, it is worth the time. If athletes do not do this at this development stage, they will run rigidly. Rigidity means higher energy expenditure and unnecessary muscle contraction that lowers velocity.

From the later stages of postpubescence, the coach has to apply annual periodization and planning. From this point on, the teacher must organize a training program to meet the needs of training for a well-defined competitive season. The coach will have a preparatory (preseason) training phase maintaining multilateral training and addressing compensation work for certain muscle groups. From late preparatory and throughout the preparatory phase, training is specific, with the coach or teacher using mostly exercises and drills that will directly improve performance. Finally, the last phase of the annual plan, transition, or off-season, training will once again be multilateral, informal, and relaxing. This is the time for removing fatigue, relaxing mentally, and maintaining some physical activity, play, and fun.

Program Design

Postpubescent speed training is more complex than what I suggest for the other two developmental phases. In addition to speed training, to meet the needs of speed and movement time development, you must train the following elements as well:

- **Speed:** High-velocity, high-frequency training, with highest intensity should be an important part of the total time dedicated to speed training.
- **Movement time:** This is elapsed time between the first overt movement of a response and completion of that movement (Anshel et al. 1991). Movement time is not only a muscular reflex to a stimulus but also the ability of the muscles to contract quickly and powerfully. Training, both speed and power, will greatly improve the ability to move a limb quickly.
- **Ability to overcome external resistance:** In most sports, power—the force of a muscle contraction—is a determinant factor in performing fast movements. During training and athletic competitions, external resistance to the athlete's quick movements exists in the form of gravity; the apparatus; the environment such as water, snow, wind, and so on; and the opponents. To defeat such opposing forces, athletes have to improve their power, so that by increasing the force of muscular contraction, they can increase the acceleration of skills. As part of training to overcome external resistance, athletes must improve the explosiveness of kicking, hitting, throwing, and batting.
- **Technique:** The speed frequency of a movement, and movement time, are often a function of technique. Acquiring a rational, effective form facilitates performing a skill quickly, correctly, and efficiently. Athletes must also give an important role to performing a skill with ease and coordination as a result of consciously relaxing the antagonistic muscles.
- **Concentration and willpower:** It seems that rapid movements are facilitated by a high degree of power. Consequently, the quickness that the central nervous system processes the athletic information coming to it, the frequency of the nervous impulses, and the athlete's maximum concentration determine the speed of a movement. The athlete's willpower and maximum concentration are important factors for achieving high speed.
- **Muscle elasticity:** Muscle elasticity and the ability to relax the agonistic and antagonistic muscles alternately are important factors in achieving high frequency of movement and correct technique. In addition, joint flexibility is an important ingredient for performing movements with high amplitude (i.e., long strides), which is paramount in any sport requiring fast running. Consequently, including daily flexibility training is imperative, especially for calf and thigh muscles.

Table 5.4 exemplifies a periodization model for speed training for postpuberty. Although the table refers to many training forms, you may select only those required in the sport of your interest.

Perform high starts standing, feet apart, in a ready position. At the signal or athlete's decision, he or she will accelerate as quickly as possible for 10 to 30 meters or yards, repeating the same action 6 to 10 times, with a three- or four-minute rest interval, when relaxation and easy stretching would maintain muscle elasticity. High starts are important for all team sports in which players are constantly in the situation to perform quick accelerations: soccer, football, baseball, hockey, lacrosse, and basketball. High starts can be performed separately from

Table 5.4   Periodization Model for Speed Training for Postpuberty

Form of training	Distance of activity (m/yd)	Number of reps and sets	Rest interval (min)	Number of speed training sessions per week
High starts	10-30	6-10	3-4	1-2
Maximum speed	20-60	4-8	3-4	2
Speed endurance	60-120	3-6	4-5	1-2
Sport-specific speed				
Accelerations	10-30	4-6	2	2-3
Decelerations	10-20	4-6	2	2
Stop and go	10-20	4-8	2	2-3
Accelerations with direction changes	10-30	4-8	2	2-3
Ballistic training (throwing, kicking, jumping, etc.)	—	2-4 sets; 5-10 reps	1-2	2-4

Note: Because these workouts are taxing, be aware of how many types of training are possible per day. Plan two to four forms of training per session, depending on the athlete's potential. The balance will be on technical or tactical work. Tables 5.5 and 5.6 give clear examples of what types of training to perform on different days of the week.

technical or tactical training in order to improve a fast start, or part of a specific drill.

Acceleration training to increase maximum speed over 20 to 60 meters or yards, four to eight times, with a rest interval of three or four minutes represents a training form that increases maximum acceleration for both sprinting and team sports. Speed endurance on the other hand, represents a form of training in which the scope is to maintain maximum velocity over a longer distance (60 to 120 meters or yards), repeated three to six times but with a longer rest interval (four or five minutes), because this type of training is taxing physically and mentally. This form of training is important for wide receivers in football, baseball players, and track athletes.

Athletes must do speed training with sport-specific forms, such as using a ball in most team sports, and so on. For team sports, deceleration, or a quick stop from fast running, is as important as the ability to accelerate maximally. Because in team sports athletes will rarely accelerate in a straight line, they must perform many sport-specific forms of training with turns, direction changes, and stop and go. The distance does not have to be long—10 to 30 meters or yards—repeated four to eight times. The rest interval is not long (two minutes) to train the athlete to be able to accelerate-decelerate not only when rested, but also in conditions of fatigue. After all, this is the case in all the team sports.

In ballistic training, athletes must perform dynamic, powerful throws, passes, kicks, hits, jumps, and so on, for example, 5 to 10 repetitions, in two to four sets, with a one- or two-minute rest interval. Most team sports use these skills, for which athletes often train under the condition of fatigue.

I must also mention two important training elements. First, athletes do not have to train all forms for all sports or in the same training session. Sprinters in track and field may perform starts and maximum speed in the same workout. However, because of its difficulty, speed endurance is trained in separate sessions from any other types of training. Wide receivers in football and baseball players would train high starts, acceleration speed, and accelerations with changes of directions in the same workout, (in the case of baseball, changes of direction mean running around the diamond). Speed endurance, on the other hand, is performed on separate days, with sport-specific form (changes of directions).

For most other team sports athletes, the forms of training can be combined in the following way.

- **1-2 days per week:** high start sprints, maximum speed training, and acceleration with changes of direction.
- **2 days per week:** acceleration and deceleration, and stop and go sprints.

The examples in table 5.5 and 5.6 further clarify this. Second, strength and power training, as suggested in chapter 6, will help the athletes to improve maximum speed and movement time.

As mentioned previously, from postpuberty on, the coach or instructor can start using annual periodization models. From this stage, athletes start to participate in more formal competitions, and training must follow a structured program. You must base such a program on the concept of periodization as in tables 5.7 through 5.9.

Looking at the models in tables 5.7 and 5.8, you can see that the progression for speed training starts from short-distance repetitions, in which the athlete seeks best form and maximum velocity for that development stage. When athletes reach this, they should progressively increase distance up to that required in the chosen sport or in a dash race.

In team sports, the longest distance that athletes must run with maximum velocity depends on the position they play in the team. For instance, wide receivers or baseball players run with maximum velocity up to 80 meters or 87 yards. In soccer, distance decreases to 40 to 60 meters or yards, whereas in basketball, the distance is not longer than 15 to 20 meters or 16 to 22 yards, unless the athlete returns to his or her own basket in the same velocity.

Irrespective of how far the athlete runs with maximum velocity, you should organize special sessions for speed training that follow the concept of periodization and incorporate elements of maximum speed, speed power, and speed endurance. These types of training programs will make an athlete a fast runner, with good acceleration.

For team sports, the ability to accelerate quickly is not sufficient. The players have to be able to change direction and decelerate quickly so they can turn around and immediately accelerate in another direction. The stronger the legs, the faster an athlete can accomplish this; therefore, an athlete should participate in strength training simultaneously with speed training.

Finally, here is a comment before I suggest some periodization models. This refers mostly to sprinters and wide receivers. In a 100-meter standard dash, you do not achieve maximum velocity at once, and it is not the same throughout the race or run. From the instant of the start, it takes an athlete four to five seconds to build up the highest speed, which depends on leg power. In fact, the analysis of a

Table 5.5	**Sample Training Plan for Maximum Acceleration—Individual Sport**						
Monday	**Tuesday**	**Wednesday**	**Thursday**	**Friday**	**Saturday**	**Sunday**
• Warm-up • Starts 6-10 times 10-30 m RI = 4 min • Power training	• Warm-up • Maximum acceleration 6 × 30 m/yd 4 × 50 m/yd 3 × 60 m/yd 4 × 30 m/yd RI = 4 min	• Warm-up • Speed endurance 4 × 60 m/yd 2 × 80 m/yd 2 × 120 m/yd 2 × 40 m/yd RI = 5 min • Power training	Off	• Warm-up • Starts: 4 × 10 m/yd 2 × 20 m/yd 2 × 30 m/yd • Maximum speed: 3 × 40 m/yd 3 × 60 m/yd RI = 4 min	• Warm-up • Speed endurance 2 × 80 m/yd 2 × 120 m/yd 4 × 60 m/yd RI = 5 min • Power training	Off

Notes: For power training, refer to chapter 6. Power training may be performed in the morning separate from speed training.

Distance expressed in m/yd.

Light stretching during RI.

RI = Rest interval.

Table 5.6	**Sample Training Plan for Maximum Acceleration—Team Sport**						
Monday	**Tuesday**	**Wednesday**	**Thursday**	**Friday**	**Saturday**	**Sunday**
• Warm-up • T drills acceleration-deceleration 10 × 30 m/yd • T drills with turns/direction changes 12 × 30 m/yd • Scrimmage RI = 2 min	• Warm-up • TA drills direction changes, stop and go 16 × 3 min • Scrimmage RI = 2 min • Ballistic training	• Warm-up • T drills maximum acceleration 6 × 15 m/yd 6 × 30 m/yd RI = 4 min • TA drills 12-14 × 1 min RI = 2 min • Ballistic training	Off	• Warm-up • T/TA drills for speed and agility 12 × 30 m/yd RI = 4 min • T/TA drills with turns, stop and go 8-10 × 1 min • Scrimmage • Ballistic training	• Warm-up • Accelerations with turns 6 × 30 m/yd • Acceleration-deceleration 8 × 30 m/yd • Stop and go 10 × 30 m/yd RI = 2 min	Off

Notes: On Saturday the program is performed individually, outside of the gym/ice arena.

Add power training on Monday, Wednesday, and Friday as per examples in chapter 6.

You may organize power training on Monday, Wednesday, and Saturday morning, separate from specific training.

T = Technical drills.

TA = Tactical drills.

100-meter dash illustrates that athletes reach peak velocity at the 50- to 60-meter mark and maintain it up to 80 meters or yards. From that point on, there is a tendency to decrease velocity. In the early part of the race, high acceleration depends on power and speed power, whereas from 70 to 80 meters on, speed endurance is required to maintain the velocity.

From this brief analysis of sprinting speed, you will observe that speed training is slightly more complicated than it may look. You must know the three segments that compose a race, what you require to perform well in all parts, and, therefore, which elements of speed you must train to become a fast runner (acceleration, maximum speed, and speed endurance). Table 5.7 illustrates a periodization model of an annual plan for speed training for a postpubescent athlete, when he or she must reach peak performance in June and July.

In the top of the chart are the months of the year and the structure of training phases. Below that are the types of speed training, distance, and percentage for a given segment of the plan. The program starts with long tempo, or a type of training in which the athlete does repetitions of 400 meters at the beginning, and 200 meters at the end, repeating this 8 to 12 times at 50 percent of maximum velocity. The scope of this type of training is developing an aerobic-anaerobic base. The same training scope is planned in the next segment of the preparatory phase (late November to mid-January), but the velocity is higher: 8 to 19 repetitions at 60 to 70 percent of maximum velocity.

On the base created during the months of October to mid-January, athletes progressively increase speed training to peak for the months of June and July. Developing maximum velocity should start from short distance in late January and February and progressively increase to full distance as competitions approach.

The distance athletes repeat to increase maximum velocity depends on the form of running. In fact, running form dictates the distance and the number of repetitions the athlete performs. In the early part of this phase, athletes repeat distances of 15 to 20 meters, requiring them to keep a relaxed and correct form. When the athletes cannot maintain form, they are fatigued, and the power of fast running is not there anymore.

When athletes can maintain the form for 30 to 40 meters, then you can plan repetitions of longer distances (40 to 60 meters), in our case from early March to mid-April. At the same time, the coach can plan low starts of short distance (10 to 15 meters) with 80 to 100 percent of maximum power and speed. Always demand a good form.

After three months of speed training with short and medium distances, the athlete can start to perform repetitions of 60 to 80 meters or yards. Focus on good form and extend the distance when athletes are to maintain maximum velocity. From this point on, throughout the competitive phase, the athletes participate in full distance or distances longer than the racing distance (overdistance) to develop maximum velocity and speed endurance.

During the months of April through July, the number of repetitions depends on how much work the athlete can tolerate and the fatigue level he or she experiences. As competitions approach, it is better to undertrain than to overtrain the athlete. Maximum velocity is possible only when the athlete is rested, fresh, and unstrained.

The lowest two rows of table 5.7 show the types of speed and power training the athlete must develop throughout the year if he or she expects to perform well in June and July.

You do not have to apply the suggested plan (table 5.7) rigidly. Climatic conditions and athletes' training potential may call for some changes. However, irrespective of changes in the plan, please follow the suggested progression and type of training.

The difference between tables 5.8 and 5.7 is that the former plan has two competitive phases: indoor competitions from January to early March and outdoor races from late May to the end of July. Between them, there are two weeks of transition in mid-March.

The progression for each peak is similar to table 5.7, except that each phase is shorter, so that two peaks are possible. All the other elements of training are similar to table 5.7.

The plan that table 5.9 illustrates has many similarities with table 5.7: the same regression regarding the training distance, from long tempo to short tempo, culminating with specific speed for August and September. During these last two months of the preparatory phase, athletes do most speed training by repeating specific technical and tactical drills, or doing speed-specific training for team sports, such as turns, changes of direction, and stop and go. This type of speed training has to train the players for a game, which is dynamic, and quick changes of speed, from jogging to maximum acceleration. The progression for power training has to support gains in specific speed for a team player that he or she must maintain throughout the league games.

You can easily adapt the example in table 5.9 to team sports in which the competitive phase is in the spring and summer months (soccer, baseball). In such a case, plan the preparatory phase for the fall and winter months and the sport-specific speed and power for March and April.

Exercises

In this chapter I present 26 exercises and games that will help young athletes develop speed and agility. These exercises (pages 81-91) are appropriate for all ages. Keep in mind that while athletes are performing the relay in this chapter, the instructor should insist on good running form (see page 69) and emphasize skills over winning.

Table 5.7 Periodization Model for Speed Training for Postpuberty

Month	Oct	Nov	Dec	Jan	Feb	Mar	Apr	May	Jun	Jul	Aug	Sep
Training phase	Preparatory								Competitive		Transition	
Types of speed training, distance, and percentage of max. velocity	Long tempo 8-12 times 400-200 m/yd at 50%		Short tempo 8-19 times 200-100 m/yd at 60-70%	Reps 20-40 m/yd 95-100%		Reps 40-60 m/yd at 95-100% Low starts of 10-15 m at 80-100%		Reps 60-80 m/yd at 90-100% Starts of 20-40 m at 90-100%		40 m/yd to full distance, or overdistance without or with starts	Other physical activities Play/games	
Speed training	Anaerobic endurance			Maximum speed		Maximum speed, maximum acceleration, speed endurance					—	
Power training	Power endurance			Starting power				Starting power, power endurance			AA	

Note: Annual plan for speed training for a postpubescent sprinter, where peak performance must be reached in June and July. AA = Anatomical adaptation

Table 5.8 Periodization Model for Speed Training for Late Postpuberty

Month	Oct	Nov	Dec	Jan	Feb	Mar	Apr	May	Jun	Jul	Aug	Sep
Training phase	Preparatory			Competitive		T	Preparatory		Competitive		Transition	
Types of speed training, distance, and percentage of max. velocity	Long tempo 400-200 m/yd at 50-60%		Short tempo 200-100 m/yd	Reps 20-40 m/yd at 95-100%	Reps 40-60 m/yd at 95-100%		Short tempo 200 m/yd at 75%	Reps 40-60 m/yd at 95-100%	Reps 60-80 m/yd at 95-100%	40 m/yd to full distance Overdistance	Other physical activities: play/games	
Speed training	Anaerobic endurance			Maximum speed Maximum acceleration		/	Anaerobic endurance	Maximum speed Maximum acceleration	Maximum acceleration Maximum speed Speed endurance			
Power training	Power endurance			Starting power		/	Power endurance	Starting power	Starting power Power endurance		AA	

Notes: Annual plan for speed training for a late postpubescent child.

T = Transition phase

AA = Anatomical adaptation

Table 5.9 Periodization Model for Speed Training for Postpuberty for a Team Sport

Month	May	June	July	August	Sept.	Oct.	Nov.	Dec.	Jan.	Feb.	March	April
Training phase	Preparatory					Competitive					Transition	
Types of speed training, distance, and % of maximum velocity	Long tempo 600 m at 50% 400 m at 60%		Short tempo 100 m-200 m at 65%	Short reps 20-30 m/yd at 90-100% Specific drills 20-90 sec at 95-100%		Maintain maximum speed and acceleration					Other physical activities play/game, outdoor activities	
Speed training	Anaerobic endurance			Maximum speed: turns, stop and go, direction changes		Maintain maximum speed using specific drills/scrimmages						
Power training	Power endurance			Power: acceleration and deceleration		Maintain power: acceleration and deceleration					AA	

Note: The league games are planned for October-January (i.e., basketball, volleyball, hockey, etc.).

FILE RELAY

Focus: running form and velocity

1. Organize a group of players in two or more relay teams of 8 to 10.

2. They stand behind the starting line, and at the instructor's signal, the first player in each file runs as fast as possible up to a cone 10 meters or yards in front of each team.

3. After turning around the cone, the player runs back toward the starting line, touching the hand of the next player in line. No player can start his or her run before touching hands.

4. Every time a player finishes running, he or she goes to the back of the line.

5. The winning team has to finish the relay faster than the others and be lined up as they started the relay.

6. You can organize file relays to perform skills such as running, carrying a ball, rolling a ball all the way, hopping, and so on.

SLALOM RELAY

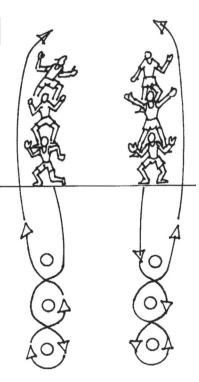

Focus: fast running with turns around cones

1. Whether using balls to roll, carry, or dribble, slalom relays have the benefit of developing running speed with turns, which is beneficial for team sports. Organize it as the file relay, except that players perform a slalom run between several cones placed in front of each team.

2. As in the file relay, players can run, dribble a ball, carry a medicine ball or any other object.

3. The rules of the file relay apply to any relay race.

FOX AND SQUIRREL

Focus: develop quickness and reaction time

1. Designate one fox and one squirrel.

2. Remaining children pair up and hold hands, facing each other with arms raised. They are designated as trees and spread out around the play area.

3. The fox chases and attempts to tag the squirrel. The squirrel can avoid being tagged by hiding in a tree. If the squirrel hides in a tree, the person facing the squirrel's back becomes the squirrel.

4. The game proceeds until each player has had a turn at being either the fox or the squirrel.

PARTNER TAG

Focus: quick reaction time and fast running around the circle

1. Designate one participant the tagger and one the first chasee. The remaining participants pair up and form a circle.

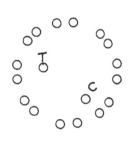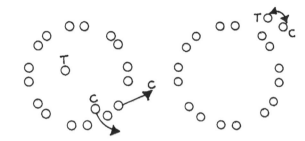

2. Tagger chases chasee. If tagger tags chasee, they reverse their roles.

3. If chasee joins a pair before being tagged, the outside pair member is now chasee.

4. If tagger begins to tire, instructor designates a new tagger.

OCTOPUS TAG

Focus: reaction time and high speed with changes of direction

1. Form a large group, with 20 to 30 participants. Designate one or two people as octopus. The remaining participants line up against one wall.

2. Octopus yell "Octopus," and participants run to opposite wall.

3. If octopus tags a participant, participant turns around on one foot to help tag others.

ARM SWING DRILL

Focus: arm drive and coordination

1. Stand with feet parallel, six inches (15 centimeters) apart. Bend elbows at 90 degrees.

2. Without changing the position of the body and elbow angle, swing the arms forward and backward. Shoulders should be down and relaxed while swinging the hands up to the level of the face.

STANDING START DRILLS

Focus: quick acceleration from standing position

1. In many sports, especially team sports, the ability to accelerate quickly is desirable. Standing start drills, therefore, train athletes to quickly start a fast acceleration in a given direction.

2. Stand with feet apart in a ready position.

3. At the instructor's signal, the player attempts to quickly accelerate in the desired direction.

Variation

Perform same with turns around a cone or a series of turns or slalom around four or five cones.

FALLING START

Focus: quick acceleration from falling forward position

1. Begin standing.

2. At commands, "On your mark," the athlete moves to the start line.

3. "Set," one foot is back, opposite arm is forward, with both arms at 90-degree angles. The body weight should be about to tip over from a slightly forward leaning position.

4. "Go," swing forward arm back vigorously and back arm forward. Drive back leg through to make first stride.

QUICK STEPS

Focus: quick acceleration with short and quick steps

1. Take either of the previous starting positions.

2. Perform quick steps from the start for 10 to 15 meters or yards, always landing the front foot below the knee of the front leg. This will result in an acceleration with short and quick steps.

HIGH KNEES

Focus: strengthens calves and hip flexors

1. Walk, driving the knee of the front leg above the horizontal, raising up on toes of the supporting leg.

2. Arms at 90 degrees drive back and forth in coordination with the legs.

3. Do repetitions of 20 to 25 meters or yards.

HARNESS RUNNING

Focus: arm drive, leg power development

1. Place a rope or ribbon around the athlete's shoulders under the armpits (like a rucksack).

2. The instructor holds the ends of the rope and opposes the athlete's forward drive with a slight resistance.

3. To defeat the resistance, the athlete has to push forcefully against the ground, slightly inclining forward, and driving the knees forward powerfully.

4. Repeat for a 10- to 15-meter or yard run.

BIG STEPS

Focus: improve leg power and long strides

1. Begin standing.

2. Make 10 to 15 marks or circles on the ground at a distance that will force the athlete to perform big steps (strides).

3. Perform long strides to always place the feet in the circles and walk back to starting point.

ACCELERATION RUN

Focus: improve fast acceleration

1. Begin standing, one leg forward, in a ready position.

2. Repeat acceleration runs observing good form: running tall, coordinating arms and legs, arms bent, heels

coming up to the buttocks, eyes forward, shoulders relaxed.

BEANBAG RELAY

Focus: acceleration, deceleration, leg power

1. Two teams line up facing each other, 65 feet (20 meters) (maximum) apart.

2. The front athlete from one team runs with the beanbag and hands it off to the front athlete of the other team, who becomes the next runner; then the first athlete sits at the back of the line.

3. The relay ends when all members have run with the beanbag and are seated.

max.20m

BEANBAG SHUTTLE

Focus: fast acceleration

1. A run and fetch game with teams running to pick beanbags out of a box.

2. The first runner takes a beanbag and places it in a box. The next player runs to the box as fast as possible, picks up the bag, and returns back to her team, giving the beanbag to the player next in line.

3. The game ends when the last team member gets a beanbag and returns to the start.

  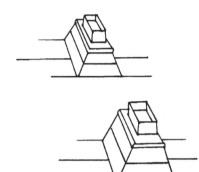

THE LOOP

Focus: start and fast run forward and around the loop

1. Divide the group into small teams of six or eight athletes. From a standing position, the athletes fall forward and start to run a loop around a cone.

2. Once around the cone they walk back rapidly.

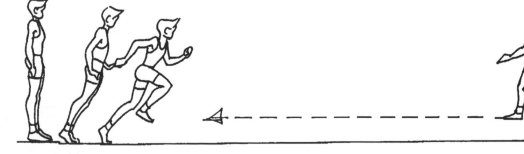 

RABBITS AND ROOSTERS

Focus: fast acceleration with quick changes of direction

1. Two teams, four meters or yards apart, each with a three-meter or yard safety zone in front of their home wall.

2. Name one team Rabbits, the other Roosters.

3. Call one team's name, then they chase the other team to their safety zone.

4. Those tagged join the other team.

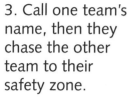

FINDERS KEEPERS

Focus: acceleration, deceleration, leg power

1. Divide the athletes into teams of four or five. Two teams 15 meters or yards apart stand to the right and behind their home hoop, which has four beanbags or balls.

2. The object is to have six beanbags in the home hoop.

3. At the start command, the first runner runs to the opposing team's hoop, finds any one of the available beanbags, picks it up, returns to the home hoop, and drops it.

4. Once the beanbag hits the floor, the second team member goes to find a beanbag in the other team's hoop.

5. End the round when a team has six bean bags.

TENTS AND CAMPERS

Focus: reaction time and acceleration

1. Athletes pair off and form one or more circles 15 to 20 meters or yards in diameter. Within each pair is a tent who stands with feet apart and a camper who sits in front of the tent.

2. The instructor calls words that begin with "t" or "c" sounds. When the instructor calls tent or camper, the appropriate member of each pair runs around the circle and either stands behind the camper or crawls into the tent.

3. Anyone moving when the instructor calls anything but tent or camper has to wait out one run.

OBSTACLE COURSE

Focus: improve leg power and run around and over obstacles

1. Set a slalom course with benches to step over, hoops to step in, mats for front rolling, and saddle horses or boxes for ducking under or climbing over.

2. Start with a walk-through and increase speed as capability increases. Leave enough room between athletes on the course (especially in doing front rolls).

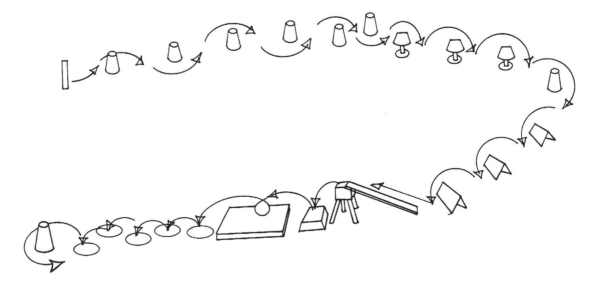

LOW OBSTACLE RELAY

Focus: acceleration and leg power

1. Set out one or more straight courses with a cone as a turnaround point. (The fewer athletes per course the better.)

2. The course should have low obstacles that athletes can run over, not leap or hop over.

3. Placing the obstacles close together encourages quick steps, and placing them farther apart encourages longer or more steps.

4. Have the athletes run the course with two steps between the obstacles; then spread them out and run it again with three or four steps between. Hurdle rhythm involves landing plus three steps between objects, like dot-dash-dash-dash in Morse code.

Note: The scope of these exercises is to improve quick footwork, which is important in many team sports.

FORWARD CROSSOVER

Focus: quick leg action and agility

1. Moving left, right leg crosses in front of left leg for 10 meters or yards in each direction.

2. Repeat.

BACKWARD CROSSOVER

Focus: quick leg action and agility

1. Moving left, right leg crosses behind left leg for five to eight meters or yards.

2. Repeat.

CARIOCA

Focus: agility and quick feet

1. Moving sideways, facing one way, forward crossover, backward crossover.

2. Repeat in both directions for 8 to 10 meters or yards.

FOOT TOUCHES

Focus: quick footwork and agility

1. Touch left hand to right heel in front of the body, then right hand to left heel in front of the body, then left hand to right heel behind the body, then right hand to left heel behind the body.

2. Repeat as quickly as possible.

Note: Simple reaction time training should be part of most activities the children perform. Their ability to react to the demands of play will result in a reaction time training effect.

GO, GO, GO, STOP

Focus: reaction time, acceleration, and deceleration

1. An athlete stands 10 meters or yards ahead of remaining participants, facing away from the group.

2. This person calls out "Go" as many times as he or she likes, then "Stop."

3. At "Go," the runners run toward the caller, and at "Stop," they freeze on the spot.

4. The caller turns to see if anyone is still moving.

5. The last person caught moving becomes the caller for the next round.

Strength and Power Training

n simple terms, strength is defined as the ability to apply force against resistance. Strength enhances the performance and execution of many athletic skills. All the skills athletes must perform against resistance will benefit from improving strength. In sports, resistance is produced by water in swimming and rowing, force of gravity in running and jumping, and by an opponent in wrestling, martial arts, or team sports.

Strength training for children has been a controversial topic. In the past, children were discouraged from using weights for fear of injury or prematurely stopping the growth process. Recent studies, however, have shown injury risk is low, and strength training may help prevent injury. Most injuries in athletics occur at the ligaments and tendons. A well-designed strength-training progression will result in strengthening the ligaments (which hold together the bones that form joints) and tendons (which anchor muscles to bones), and as a result, allow the athlete to better cope with the strain of training and competitions. Strength training not only helps prevent injuries now but also provides a strong foundation for the later stages of high-performance athletes.

Another misconception about strength training is that it applies only to bodybuilders or power lifters. As demonstrated in the past two decades, many athletes have improved their performance faster using strength training than just performing the skill of the chosen sport. Strength training is an integral part of many athletes' training: football, baseball, track and field, rowing and canoeing, wrestling, tennis, and so on. Now the philosophy has so drastically changed that some people believe no one can be fast before being strong, no one can increase the height of a jump or takeoff without strength training, and no one can throw

93

or shoot a ball without having strong arms. Indeed, strength training has gained its important role in most sports.

In addition to improving performance and being a safeguard against injuries, strength training has health benefits. As a direct result of strength training, the mineral content of the bones increases serving later in life as a preventative measure against osteoporosis. According to medical data, women are more prone to osteoporosis, therefore strength training should be part of the physical education and training program of young girls (Committee for the Development of Sport of the Council of Europe, 1982). The benefit of strength training can also be social and psychological, in which training enhances an individual's discipline and mental determination to accomplish a task. Furthermore, a strong person seems to have high self-esteem and confidence. Finally, strength training has to be part of a lifestyle and healthy living, because by increasing the body's proportion of lean muscle mass, it also increases metabolism and in the process burns more calories than a sedentary lifestyle.

Strength training can be a positive component of a child's active lifestyle; however, you must carefully design it for a specific age or sport (Bar-Or and Goldberg 1989; Bompa, 1993a). Before participating in a strength-training program, young athletes must be ready physically and psychologically, and must understand the technique and role of strength in performance improvement. Both the instructor and the child should be aware of safety factors, including spotting and how to use different types of equipment. Equally important is that the supervising instructor is competent in the area of strength training, both in the technique of lifting and training methodology.

Before beginning a strength-training program, a child should have a thorough medical examination. This will determine any potential illness (such as heart problems) that may prevent the child from doing strength training or any type of physical training. With clearance from a physician, children with certain physical or mental disabilities can participate in a safe and professionally conducted strength-training program.

Terminology

The literature uses several terms interchangeably—weight training, resistance training, power training, or strength training. Because you can develop strength without weights or applying force against resistance, I have selected the term strength training to express force produced by a group of muscles.

You can also combine strength with other factors such as speed or endurance. In the first case, strength and speed result in *power,* or the rate at which you can generate force. This is usually fast, with explosiveness, such as in batting or jumping. The second combination, strength and endurance, is called *muscular endurance,* which results in the ability to perform many repetitions against a resistance, as in rowing, swimming, and cycling.

A group of muscles perform the sport skills. The larger and more powerful muscles, primarily responsible for performing technical skills, are called *prime movers.* Other muscles that cooperate in accomplishing the movement are called *synergist muscles. Antagonist muscles,* which are mainly on the opposite side of the bone, act in opposition to the synergists. All the motions are, therefore, influenced by give and take, by the contraction of synergists (also called *agonists*), and a balanced and controlled relaxation of the antagonists.

While an athlete is performing a motion with this critical interaction between agonists and antagonists, the role of other groups of muscles is to support a limb so the needed muscles can produce the motion. During pitching, for instance, the abdominal muscles contract to fix the lower part of the trunk so the arms can throw the ball. These supporting muscles are called fixators, or stabilizers, because they keep one part of the body or limb stable while another part contracts to perform a motion.

The load in strength training is expressed in pounds or kilograms and calculated in percentage of one repetition maximum (1RM), or the highest load you can lift in one repetition. You can easily test this as exemplified in a bench press. To find 1RM, the athlete can start with a small load, say 60 pounds. If the athlete lifts this easily, then make the next load heavier (i.e., 80 pounds, etc.). The highest load the athlete lifts in one repetition is called 1RM or 100%. Use this load to calculate the percentage for training, in most cases between 30 and 95 percent of 1RM.

The *number of repetitions* refers to how many times to repeat an exercise in a set. The following guideline will assist you:

- For a load of 100 percent, perform just one repetition.
- If the load is 95 percent, two or three repetitions are possible.
- At 90 percent of 1RM, three or four repetitions are possible.
- For a load of 85 percent, an athlete can do five or six repetitions.
- If the load is 80 percent, an athlete can do 8 to 10 repetitions.
- For a load of 75 percent, an athlete normally performs 12 repetitions.
- For 70 percent of 1RM, an athlete can lift 12 to 15 repetitions.
- Between 60 and 70 percent, a trained athlete can easily perform 18 to 20 repetitions.
- If the load is 50 percent, an athlete can perform more than 25 repetitions per set.

During a strength-training session, young athletes can perform one or two sets per exercise. Late postpuberty athletes can go beyond that, up to three, but in a progressive way, and increasing the number of sets over two to four years. For young athletes, there is no reason to perform more than two or three sets. In doing so, the number of exercises have to be low, six or seven exercises.

Between sets always take a rest interval (RI) to rest and relax muscles before performing the next exercise. The suggested programs will always have a rest interval of two or three minutes.

Laws of Strength Training

Three basic laws for the foundation of strength training should underlie a good strength-training program. These rules apply to anyone involved in strength training during the stages of growth and development, but are especially important to the young athlete who has just started along the road to high performance.

Law One: Develop Joint Flexibility

Most strength-training exercises, especially those employing free weights, use the whole range of motion of major joints, particularly knees, ankles, and hips.

For example, in deep squats the weight of the barbell compresses the knees and may cause strain and pain if the athlete does not have good flexibility at the knee joint. If deep knee squats are used in children's training, the load must be very low in order to avoid strain.

In a low squat position, the lack of good ankle flexibility forces the performer to stay on the balls of the feet and toes, rather than on the flat of the feet, which ensures a good base of support and balance. Therefore, developing good ankle flexibility during prepubescence and pubescence must be a major concern. Consequently, athletes seek flexibility development as an injury prevention strategy as well as for its own merits. Start during prepubescence and pubescence and maintain in later stages of athletic development.

Law Two: Develop Tendon Strength Before Muscle Strength

Muscle strength always improves faster than the tendons' abilities to withstand tension and the ligaments' resistance to preserve the integrity of the bones forming the joints. Faulty use of the principle of specificity and the lack of a long-term vision cause many training specialists and coaches to constantly stress just the specific exercises for a given sport. Consequently, they do not pay attention to the overall strengthening of ligaments, particularly at an early age when time is not pressing.

Athletes strengthen tendons and ligaments through a program designed to attain *anatomical adaptation* (to progressively adapt the anatomy of young athletes), and I discuss it in this chapter. Tendons attach the muscles to bones. Their main function is to transmit the pull or force that muscle contraction generates against the bone, which moves a given joint. Vigorous strength training without proper anatomical adaptation of tendons and ligaments can result in injuries of muscle attachments (tendons) and joints (ligaments). Tendons and ligaments are trainable, resulting in their enlargement (increase in diameter) increasing their ability to withstand tension and tearing.

Law Three: Develop Core Strength Before Limbs

The result of misunderstanding the principle of specificity is that training specialists direct most of their attention toward developing arms and legs. This misunderstanding is because athletes play most sports with the arms and legs. Therefore many trainers concentrate on strengthening these two segments of the body, believing that the stronger they are the more effective they will be.

Although it is true that legs and arms are the performers of all athletic skills, the trunk is the link between them. The legs and arms are only as strong as the trunk! A poorly developed trunk leads to a weak support for the hardworking arms and legs.

Long-term strength-training programs should not revolve on only the arms and legs of the body, but should include the abdominals, lower back, and spinal column musculature. Consequently, when preparing training programs for young athletes, especially during prepubescence and pubescence, exercises should start from the core section of the body and work toward the extremities. In other words, before strengthening the legs and arms, concentrate on developing the link between them, the support, the core muscle groups of the trunk.

The abdominal and back musculature provides the trunk with an array of muscles, whose bundles run in different directions and surround the core area of the body. This provides a tight and powerful support for the wide range of physical moves.

Back muscles are the long and short muscles that run along the vertebral column and work with the rotator and diagonal muscles as a unit, taking part in sideways bending, turning the trunk, and rotating.

Abdominal muscles are the anterior, lateral, and obliques that can pull in opposite directions through fibers that cross the abdominal wall. This enables the trunk to bend forward, sideways, rotate, and twist. The abdominals play important roles in many sport skills; therefore, weak abdominal muscles can restrict the effectiveness of athletes in many activities.

All trunk muscles can work as a unit to stabilize and keep the trunk fixed during movements of the arms and legs, especially in throwing activities from baseball to track and field.

Adapting Strength Training for Young Athletes

Scientific studies have demonstrated that both boys and girls gain in strength following strength training (Bar-Or and Goldberg, 1989; Micheli, 1988; Ramsay et al., 1990; Sale, 1986). Comparisons of children in all three stages of growth and development (prepubescence, pubescence, and postpubescence) show that postpubescent children make the greatest gains. This is often as much as two or three times that of prepubescent children and almost twice that of pubescent children.

Most gains in postpubescent children are the result of growth in muscle mass (hypertrophy), as well as nonmuscular factors, such as neuromuscular or nervous system adaptation to training. Although strength gains are visible in prepubescent and pubescent children, gains in muscle mass are not. Strength improvements in early age are not, therefore, the result of muscle enlargement (hypertrophy) but rather the ability of the central nervous system (CNS) to activate or stimulate the muscles (Bompa, 1993a; Sale, 1986). We see this in the improved ability of children to perform a skill efficiently and with force and power. Consequently, most muscles learn to cooperate, synchronizing their actions and contracting the chain of muscles involved in strength training. The result is increased force in the intended direction of movement.

Strength gains for male athletes during postpuberty and maturation are mostly the result of muscle enlargement due to the large increments, from puberty on, of male hormone (testosterone). Female athletes cannot report similar gains during these periods because their testosterone levels are tenfold lower than in the male counterpart (Fox, Bowers, and Foss 1989). Even nonathletic males increase their strength and size markedly compared with females, for the same biological reason. As a consequence, athletes increase trainability of strength rapidly during puberty and maintain it during the following development stages.

Considerations for Prepuberty

The prepuberty years are characterized by a constant growth that favors developing fundamental movements and basic skills. Individual variations in motor performance among children are so diverse that they can change over a short time. Certainly heredity, the natural qualities children inherit from their parents, plays an important role in individual performances and their variations (Matsui, 1983).

Physique and strength are generally related for boys; overall body size influences physical achievements. Excess body fat, however, plays an adverse role in most motor activities.

Physical achievements increase markedly and linearly with age, but gender differences in average strength (particularly lower body strength) do not seem to be drastically different. Boys seem to do better in strength-related activities for the upper body, such as throws, relative to activities of the lower body, such as sprinting. Girls tend to perform better in balance and flexibility (Duda, 1986; Smith, 1984).

Considerations for Puberty

Motor performance improves with age during puberty, but the development pattern is not uniform for the same age, sex, and task (Malina, 1984). For girls, strength performance levels off during puberty and does not visibly change afterward. For boys, strength increases with age at an average rate, with marked acceleration during growth spurts, when there are also visible increments in muscle mass. This probably reflects gains in testosterone level and a social factor, because for boys peer pressure seems to motivate them to look bigger and be stronger. Because large increments in muscle size are not possible, especially during early puberty, it is important for everyone involved in children's sports to discourage young athletes from taking part in strength training solely to create big muscles. Such gains will be possible only after hormonal changes have occurred during this growth stage, because increments in muscle mass parallel sex organ development (Bailey, Malina, and Mirwald, 1985).

From puberty on, boys are significantly stronger than girls in upper body and arms. There appears to be a lesser difference for leg strength. In general terms, strength visibly relates to body size and fat-free muscle mass, which gives boys the advantage because they tend to participate in more physical activities than girls (Kraemer and Fleck, 1993).

Regarding power, tests such as the standing long jump show similar performances for boys and girls during prepuberty, but from puberty on these gender differences in power change visibly. At the same time, gains in excess body fat for some girls appear to lower their performance proficiency.

Considerations for Postpuberty

Postpuberty signals a large difference in motor performance relative to gender. During adolescence, the difference between girls and boys seems to accelerate in tasks and performances related to strength due to boys' adolescent growth spurt. From this stage on, few girls perform as well as boys in strength, which was possible during prepuberty. These differences reflect sex differences, especially because boys grow larger in size. Social and motivational factors are important considerations in interpreting children's performances, with involvement in physical activities being directed more toward boys than girls.

Some boys decline in performance during peak height increases in growth spurts. Often children at this stage grow 5 to 10 centimeters (two to four inches) per year, which obviously affects performance. This is especially true for girls, who experience a greater decrease in strength due to growth and leverage changes (Bailey, Malina, and Mirwald, 1985; Kraemer and Fleck, 1993; Micheli, 1988). Following this phase of fast growth in height, most strength and power scores start to improve again, demonstrating good adaptability to challenging training loads. On top of this, peer pressure to be strong and look big makes it difficult for some boys to resist the temptation to use drugs that increase muscle size. This is when it is necessary for parents, educators, and coaches to explain the danger of drugs and to demonstrate that there are better alternatives, such as the periodization of strength training.

It becomes evident that some children grow faster (early maturers) than others of the same age (late maturers). Girls who experience menarche at an early age (during puberty) are slightly stronger than those who attain it later. By the time girls reach postpuberty, early maturers are less strong than late maturers because of gains in relative body fat, combined with decreased activity in the upper-body region. Early maturers tend to be heavier and taller than late maturers. Their upper body and abdominals are weaker because they grow more quickly. Their strength in relation to body size decreases because of quicker growth spurts, compared with late maturers. When the growth spurt is over, and training gains

become visible again, early maturers seem to have a strength advantage over late maturers. This is particularly so in the legs, the strength of which girls sometimes retain during maturation.

Early maturing boys perform better than average and late maturers. Average maturing boys increase linearly until late adolescence. From this stage of development on, there are negligible differences in strength performance between early and average maturing boys. Boys who reach early sexual maturation, however, perform better in strength-related movements (Borms and Hebbelinck, 1984; Malina, 1984). Later maturers, on the other hand, rarely catch up with early maturers in most strength power-related motor tasks. Again, body size seems to significantly influence performance. However, later phases of athletic development (high performance) may not retain any advantages or disadvantages of the early growth and development stages). It is important, therefore, to understand and follow a long-term periodization of athletic development, which guarantees a gradual and complete development of the abilities necessary for all sports.

In conclusion, training programs for children have to consider the dynamics of growth and development for each stage. Programs for both boys and girls should be similar and well-balanced for the first two development stages, but completely separate for postpuberty. As part of a well-rounded training concept, strength plays a major factor for general fitness. To maintain proportional strength between the upper and lower body in girls, from puberty and especially postpuberty on, programs should emphasize upper-body, trunk, and shoulder girdle strength, because they tend to be weaker in these areas.

Preventing Injuries

Children may experience injuries by lifting heavy weights during their growth, especially during prepuberty and puberty. Children, especially prepubescents, cannot activate their muscles as adults do and are therefore more prone to certain injuries than adults (Fleck and Falkel, 1986; Rovere, 1988). A lack of knowledge in training and appropriate load progression, improper posture during lifting, and weak abdominal muscles are in most cases the culprits for children's injuries. Young athletes experience lower back problems and knee injuries.

Growth plate injuries, compression injuries in the shaft of the bones, are the most serious injuries. A growth plate fracture during childhood may result in shortness of a limb. These injuries occur most often in contact sports. Young children are extremely susceptible to serious damage from sudden violent forces because the ligaments that protect major joints are stronger than the growth plates. Consequently, trauma that would cause ligament damage in adults will often cause growth plate fractures in children.

Muscle overload can also create serious injuries in children. Extreme muscle contractions transmitted along the tendons, which can cause muscle tearing in adults, can cause the muscle and tendon to separate from the main structure of the bone in children. If such injuries stop growth the result could be deformity and functional impairment.

Injuries such as strains, sprains, and soft tissue damage are far more common and yet much more difficult to prevent than growth plate injuries. These injuries occur frequently in highly organized competitive sports programs. Although they are not necessarily serious, they can slow the overall development of athletic talent.

A well-structured strength-training program, a well-designed long-term periodization, like the ones I present in this chapter, is safe for children. Following the suggested programs is a key assurance against injuries. It is equally important to know that bigger, stronger children, especially during late puberty and postpuberty, are more likely to experience injuries. They feel ready for heavy loads. What these young adults misunderstand, however, is that the ossification process is not yet completed, and as a result, muscles should not pull against connective tissue with maximum force.

Among the most effective injury-prevention techniques are the following:

- Use strength-training programs designed to prevent injuries. A well-planned and long anatomical adaptation phase, as suggested by the models, can result in building injury-free athletes. Athletes who do not experience any weight-training program have a three to one injury rate compared with those who do.

- Design a compensation strength-training program for all muscles, especially for the abdomen, to balance the strength of the lower back and the rotator cuffs, to avoid shoulder pain. These tend to be the neglected areas in training.

- Do not abuse specificity in training programs for children by using constant exercises specific for the sport. Multilateral training at an early age will pay off at maturation. Specificity of training at an early age has a greater chance in creating overuse injuries.

- Do not expose athletes to maximum loads over 70 to 80 percent of 1RM or explosive lifts with free weights during prepuberty, puberty, and early postpuberty. This is too strenuous for anyone, let alone for a young body with an immature anatomical development. In fact, *discomfort should not be part of the early years of training, period!*

- Thorough instruction in lifting techniques, especially free weights, must be part of any strength-training program. An adequate phase of learning lifting technique, with no or light weights, is a logical requirement by any instructor with a long-term vision.

- Close supervision at all times is necessary for a problem-free gym. Children, especially prepubescent and pubescent, have short attention spans and are not necessarily highly motivated for strength training; therefore, you should constantly guide and supervise them. Have equipment serviced regularly, and always return weights to their safe place.

- Never use faulty or worn equipment. Before lifting with free weights, such as barbells, make sure that the collars are secured to prevent the discs from falling off and harming the body.

Circuit Training

You can use simple circuit training (named as such because the stations are organized in a circle) with six to nine stations, to develop basic strength by using exercises listed on pages 116-148. Tables 6.1 and 6.2 are provided as examples. Consider the following characteristics of organizing a circuit training program:

- Training should last between 15 and 20 minutes. You can progressively increase it to 30 minutes toward the end of prepuberty.

- Arrange the exercises so they alternate limbs, body parts, and muscle groups. I suggest the following order for the exercises: legs, arms, abdomen, and back.

- The number of exercises is between six and nine.

- For new exercises, the coach must teach the proper technique. Correct execution should take priority over the number of repetitions.

- The instructor should not demand a certain speed or have the children complete an exercise or circuit as fast as possible. At this stage of development, these things are not important. For children to enjoy performing a circuit of exercises, they must do them *at their own speed*.

- The movements should look smooth. Children should be able to perform them without experiencing discomfort. A grimace is a sign of discomfort with a stressful activity. At this stage of development stress is categorically undesirable. Where there is stress there is no fun! Stop any activity before children experience discomfort. Do not push! Let children have a positive physical experience.

- As much as possible, introduce exercises into the circuit that are enjoyable, fun, and that the children will be interested in performing.

- Provide constant rewards and encouragement for good technique and individual improvement. Circuit training should be an environment for individual improvement, challenge, and personal satisfaction, and not competition between children. However, children should know from the beginning that they cannot expect improvements all the time and for all exercises and activities. The road to a good performance is full of gratification and frustration, and constant improvement is not always the case. Consistent and persistent work, however, is always rewarded in the long run.

Remember that during prepubescence, children should *not lift heavy loads*. No child should attempt to know how much they can lift, their maximum weight, or one repetition maximum. The medical and scientific professionals strongly

Table 6.1	**Circuit Training With Six Exercises**	
Exercises	Number of reps/duration in sec	Rest interval (sec)
• Push-up	4 - 6 (8)	30
• MB scoop throw	10 - 12 (15)	30
• Dumbbell curl	8 - 10 (12)	30
• Hang hip flexion	5 - 8	60
• Dumbbell shoulder press	8 - 12	30
• Two leg skip	60 sec	120

Note: Depending on the abilities of the athletes involved, a child may perform 1-2 circuits and toward the end of puberty even 3 circuits.

MB = Medicine ball

Table 6.2	Circuit Training With Nine Exercises	
Exercises	Number of reps/duration in sec	Rest interval (sec)
• Push up	6 - 8 (10)	30
• Hip thrust	6 - 10	30
• Single-leg burpee	8 - 10/leg	60
• MB trunk raise	6 - 8	30
• MB scoop throw	10 - 12 (15)	30
• Abdominal crunch	6 - 8	30
• Dodge the rope	60 sec	60
• Dumbbell curl	8 - 10 (12)	30
• Loop skip	90 sec	120

Note: Start with one circuit and over time progressively increase to two, then to three.

discourage using heavy loads (especially with free weights) during childhood, particularly during prepubescence and pubescence, due to possible growth plate injuries (American Academy of Pediatrics, 1983).

The exercises and training characteristics I suggested previously are adequate to build the base for future phases of strength development. With the activities children perform during puberty, they will build the foundation for the training to come during adolescence and maturation. To do it any other way would mean burnout for the young athletes, and they will lose interest in sports before they reach their best performance levels at physical and psychological maturation.

Periodization Models for Strength

Table 6.3 refers to a long-term periodization model for strength. It is an overview, which refers to the development stages, training method, volume (quantity), intensity (load), and means of training.

Strength-Training Model for Initiation

View the suggested model for prepuberty as preparatory time in which the athlete develops the foundation for high performance in an enjoyable, fun, and playful environment. High performance at athletic maturation does not depend on strength training during prepubescence. The body at this stage is susceptible to injury with excessive stress. Regimented, stressful strength training using machines not only puts prepubescent athletes at serious risk for injury, but also leads to burnout and hurts the careers of potential high performers. Therefore, you should view strength training for prepubescent children only as an additive to the technical work and general skill development, and limit it to the athlete's body weight or medicine ball exercises.

Table 6.3	**Periodization Model for Long-Term Strength Training**				
Stages of development	Forms of training	Training methods	Volume	Intensity	Means of training
Initiation	• Simple exercises • Games/play	• Informal circuit training (CT)	• Low	• Very low	• Own body • Partners • Light medicine balls
Athletic formation	• General strength • Relays/games	• CT	• Low to medium	• Low	• Medicine ball • Light free weights
Specialization	• General strength • Specificity	• CT • Power training • Low impact plyometrics	• Medium • Medium-high • Maximum	• Low • Medium Submaximum	• As above • Free weights
High performance	• Specificity	• Maximum strength • Power/plyometrics • Muscular endurance	• Medium • Medium-high • Maximum	Medium to high Submaximum	• Free weights • Other types of machines

Note: The progression in training methods, volume, intensity, and especially the cautious transition from simple exercises (initiation) to general, then to specific.

Remember that multilateral development is the major scope of training for prepuberty. By playing sports (the more varied the better), children develop basic strength, general endurance, basic speed of short distance, and good coordination. For instance, if a child participates in a recreational swimming program, he or she can also take a few gymnastics classes to develop basic flexibility and balance. While playing games, a young athlete is also developing endurance, speed, coordination, agility, and space orientation and performing a variety of skills. This multitude of skills will result in a harmonious physical development rather than a sport-specific narrowness.

Although children spend most of the time performing the chosen sport, play, and games, they should dedicate 20 to 30 percent of their training time per week to physical training, from strength to flexibility. They should perform such a program informally, free from regimentation and rigidity and full of enjoyment and fun.

You should see the whole strength-training program for prepubescent and pubescent athletes as adapting the anatomy of children to prepare the muscles, tendons, and joints for the training stress of high performance at maturation. The aim of the program is overall, harmonious, and proportional body development, as called for in the principle of multilateral development. During the stages of growth and development, six to eight years of progressive development, the athletes should prepare so they are injury free in the later development stages. This requires a careful progression in the program.

When creating a plan, give attention to the training guidelines, such as multilateral development, individualization of any program and exercises, and a progressive load increment, discussed in chapter 1.

Strength-Training Model for Athletic Formation

You should view a training program for pubescence as continuing to build the foundation of training necessary for an athlete to specialize in a sport. Such a base is paramount for the success many athletes aspire to during the high-performance phase. Therefore, view puberty as an important stage in the equation for producing high-quality athletes.

Although pubescent children grow rapidly during this stage, sometimes 10 to 12 centimeters (4 to 5 inches) per year, adequate strength training is essential for the young athletes. The intensity of the loads used for training should still be low, because hard training during pubescence may affect normal growth and contribute to injuries (Matsuda et al., 1986).

From puberty on, boys and girls will have different gains from strength training. The development of sexual organs in boys results in high levels of growth hormones (some 10 times higher levels of testosterone than girls). For this reason, boys get bigger and stronger than girls.

Scope of Training

You should view strength training as part of overall development. Multilateral training or developing a high variety of skills and basic motor abilities, such as flexibility, endurance, and speed, is still an important goal.

For strength training, the aim of the program is a proportional and harmonious body and musculature development. Except sports in which athletes achieve high performance during late puberty and early adolescence, resist falling into the trap of specificity. Do not stress training methods and especially do not employ exercises specific for selected sports only. Stressing specificity at this early stage will mean rapid adaptation, causing the athletes to reach good performance at an unnecessarily young age. As children improve fast, the temptation increases to push them higher, use heavier loads, and demand better performance. This stress in training is often exacerbated by entering the young athlete into more and difficult competitions. The result of this approach can be predictable: high stress and burnout. The goal of strength training in pubescence is to further the base of strength for the high-performance phase. As was demonstrated during the 1992 and 1996 Olympic Games, most medalists were in their late 20s and early 30s. Consequently, avoid specificity; work for multilateral development; build a solid base for the future; and most importantly, create an environment that is fun, enjoyable, and a positive physical experience. Remember the Roman dictate, *Festina lente,* which means hurry up slowly!

Program Design

A strength-training program designed for pubescence should continue to apply the three basic laws of strength training. Do further work on developing joint flexibility, strengthening the tendons, and improving the core area of the body.

Developing a good strength base, with harmonious muscles, is a major goal of strength training at this stage. This will prepare the athletes anatomically for the training stress they will meet during postpubescence and maturation. The direct benefit of such long-term progression is creating injury-free athletes. With good progression this is a possibility.

A training program for pubescence represents an advanced link with training for high performance. Although you may employ similar means of training using the same types of equipment, such as exercises requiring your body weight and a partner, the number of repetitions and resistance will be slightly more challenging. Continue exercises with medicine balls, mostly throws and relays. Seek the foundation of power using the athlete's body weight, and develop speed and power by using medicine balls. Increase the weight of the ball slightly, from two to four kilograms (five to nine pounds). Use exercises with dumbbells and wall pulleys to develop the strength base and adapt the tendons and ligaments.

Because they are slightly increasing the total amount of work, children will experience some fatigue. This will be especially true if they perform skills of a given sport and 30 minutes of circuit training for strength development in the same day. Cease activity before feeling pain. The instructor should constantly observe the young athletes and learn how much they can tolerate before they feel discomfort.

A sign of comfortable physical exertion is that training still looks effortless. To achieve this, children should focus on the task while being relaxed, to prevent muscle strain. They should understand that, although the agonistic muscles contract, the antagonists should relax.

At this stage of training, children can experience free weights with light and simple barbells available in most gyms. However, this does not mean Olympic weightlifting techniques. Rather it is for them to learn what kinds of exercises they can perform with a barbell. The main reason for suggesting barbells and not sophisticated machines is that athletes can perform a greater variety of movements in different positions and planes. Using a barbell, it is easier to mimic a skill pattern that an athlete will perform during postpubescence and maturation. Before thinking about training, however, the instructor should thoroughly teach correct lifting techniques. This is crucial to avoid possible injuries. Most gym machines are not designed for the length of children's limbs.

Consider the following key elements for basic technical instructions:

• Teach basic stance, with feet parallel at shoulder width. This position will guarantee a good support base, giving the child controlled balance. This means that as a child performs, for example, upright rowing, he or she will not lose balance.

• Lead the lift with neck and shoulders. For example, when lifting the barbell from the floor to the chest or shoulders (this is called clean), the athlete should concentrate on starting and leading the move with the neck and shoulders. Do not focus on the barbell, it will follow the upper body lead. Flex the arms in the second half of the action. This technique will eliminate the error of shooting the legs (leading with the hips and, therefore, leaving the upper body behind); such errors can result in lower back strains.

Most concerns should address multijoint movements, such as the previous one, or performing a half squat. Because half or deeper squats are popular exercises, the progression of teaching is as follows:

1. Learn the correct technique without any weight (free squats).

2. Learn to balance up the barbell you will use in the future by placing a stick on the shoulders, with hands toward the ends of the stick.

3. Go through the motion using dumbbells, one in each hand, and lifting them on the sides of the body.

4. Use just a barbell with no additional weights attached.

5. Use slightly increased loads while concentrating on a correct technique.

If an instructor is not aware of the correct technique, he or she should learn this from a specialist. In any case, understand that this progression is a long-term proposition. It usually takes a couple years before the athlete uses a heavier load and, normally, this is in late postpuberty.

As children develop a better training background, they should progressively experience slightly more challenging training demands, meaning skills for technical development, speed, agility, and strength. In this way, their adaptation will reach higher ceilings, illustrated by their growing capacity to tolerate work and progressively increase their physical potential. To achieve this, the total training demand has to progressively increase following a certain methodology, such as the following:

1. Increase the duration of a training session. Assume that training is twice a week for one hour. To slightly increase the training capacity, the instructor adds 15 minutes to each session. Now the child will train twice at 75 minutes, for an additional 30 minutes per week. Over time, such progressive increments may go up to 90 minutes per session. The 90-minute session does not mean just strength training. It includes technical and tactical work; speed; agility; and, toward the end of the session, strength training.

2. Increase the number of training sessions per week. Considering that a 90-minute session is long enough for training, a new training challenge will come from increasing the number of sessions from two to three per week.

3. Increase the number of repetitions per training sesson for all types of activities and skills, such as technical, tactical, and physical. If for a certain period the coach feels that three times at 90 minutes per week is what the children can tolerate, the next training increment will come from performing more work in the 90 minutes. This means more technical drills or exercises for physical development. Consequently, slightly decrease the rest interval between drills, and challenge the children to adapt to high training demands.

4. Increase the number of repetitions of skills and drills per set. When you exhaust the previous three options, higher training demand will come from increasing the number of repetitions of drills or exercises performed per set. In this way, the new training task is to progressively adapt a child to perform the increased number of repetitions nonstop, without a rest interval between them.

You must apply this proposed progression carefully, over a long time. It may take two or three years to increase the training load from two 60-minute sessions a week to three 90-minute sessions a week. An experienced instructor will certainly make a smooth and careful transition.

The strength-training increment can be from 20 to 30 and even 40 minutes per session toward the end of pubescence. The circuit-training method still satisfies the needs of strength development, except that the number of exercises can increase progressively up to 10 or 12, with 8 to 15 repetitions per exercise.

Strictly adhere to individualization so that training programs match individual potential. Similarly, the speed of performing an exercise must be a child's natural choice, without additional pressure from the instructor. This allows the child to find his or her way, according to individual rhythm of growth and development, which can be drastically different between two children of the same age.

The instructor may use rewards as a motivational tool. However, give any rewards (i.e., praise for achieving a task) for individual self-improvement rather than for being the best athlete in the group.

During pubescence, children should experience various track and field events, with lowered weight for throwing implements (i.e., use tennis balls rather than javelin), and shortened distance for sprinting (50 meters or 55 yards rather than 100 meters or 110 yards). The advantage of learning basic skills, and developing speed and power, is that later there will be a valuable positive transfer, for example, from javelin throw to pitching in baseball or from good sprinting abilities to football, basketball, or soccer. Therefore, the multilateral base for prepubescence and puberty is not just a concept to be concerned with, but an athletic necessity for high performance.

Training Program

A strength-training program for puberty can successfully use the circuit-training method. You can use tables 6.1 and 6.2 with circuits of six and nine exercises as training guidelines. Parents or instructors can easily create other programs using many of the following exercises. Please adjust the number of repetitions and the number of circuits according to the potentials of the children in the program.

Strength-Training Model for Specialization

From postpuberty on, the training program changes slightly, compared with the first two growth and development stages, when the major scope was multilateral. With the foundation athletes create during prepubescence and pubescence, training for postpubescence becomes progressively specific to the needs of the selected sport. With such a background, strength training diversifies to include power and to progressively use the periodization model for each competitive year.

As a result of increasing growth hormones, mostly for boys, muscle size and strength will be noticeably larger during postpubescence. From this stage of development up to maturation, boys will increase the proportion of muscles from approximately 27 percent to about 40 percent of total body mass. Under such circumstances, strength will certainly improve drastically. Although this will be slightly different for girls, they will also improve their strength to much higher levels (Hebbelinck, 1989; Malina, 1984).

Scope of Training

Postpubescence is a development phase that includes young athletes with a difference in chronological age of two or three years. Therefore, you must carefully and progressively monitor the introduction of training specificity according to the needs of the sport.

Maintain multilateral training during postpubescence, although you will progressively alter the proportions between it and sport-specific training in favor of specificity. Of equal importance is maintaining work for strength improvements and functionality of the core area of the body.

You should view specificity of strength training as incorporating exercises that mimic the motion the prime movers (agonistic muscles) perform. The athlete must angle and plane the motion specifically to the technical skills of the selected sports. However, you should implement specificity so it does not disturb the harmonious development of the other muscles (antagonists).

Because strength training diversifies to address the specific needs of a sport, the athlete will develop different components of strength, such as power and muscular endurance. Employ specific training methods to address such needs. As a direct result, you must also understand and implement periodization of strength per competitive year.

Program Design

Following the first one or two years of postpubescence, when pubescent-specific training still applies, training becomes progressively sophisticated. You may use additional training methods and more sophisticated training machines.

As training becomes more complex and strength plays an important role, you should monitor the stress in training. As athletes add more power and heavier loads, training intensity takes a toll through the fatigue they are experiencing. To prevent a critical level of fatigue and potential injury, the instructor should know how to increase the intensity in strength training appropriately. I suggest the following progression:

1. Decrease the rest interval between sets from 3 minutes to 2.5 minutes.
2. Increase the number of sets per training session, especially for the higher percentage of 1RM.
3. Increase the training load. According to the principle of progressive increase of load in training, increase the load in steps, usually three, followed by a regeneration week (refer to chapter 1 for an explanation of the step method). To adapt to the new load, the athlete must maintain a training program of similar intensity for approximately a week, followed by a new load increment.

Figure 6.1 illustrates a hypothetical load increment over four weeks. The training load increases from step to step by approximately 10 percent, except the regeneration week when it decreases by 20 percent. Please note that the load per step refers to the training program for one day, which the athlete must repeat two or three times, depending on the number of training sessions per week.

Apply this progression over a long time. In doing this, it is normal to expect that athletes will use high percentages, close to 100 percent, at the end of postpubescence and

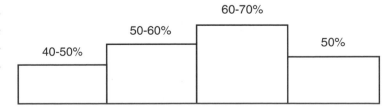

Figure 6.1 Percent increase of training load for a four-week cycle.

during maturation. Similarly, you can increase the number of sets to two, four, or higher to challenge the muscles for adaptation and improvement.

As the complexity of training increases, you may be tempted to employ sophisticated strength machines or Olympic weightlifting moves, such as clean and jerks and snatch, with the belief that by doing them, strength for the selected sport will quickly improve. I strongly discourage using these methods, as they are technical, sometimes dangerous, and not sport specific.

The market offers other types of machines in addition to the universal gym. Among them are the following:

- Variable resistance machines, which vary the resistance to match the dynamics of an exercise. With these, the prime movers can contract maximally or near maximally throughout the range of movement.
- Isokinetic machines, which have a system that makes the speed of exertion constant throughout the range of movement.

Although these and other machines might be ideal for providing resistance to some muscles, the problem is that they allow the movement to occur only in a predetermined direction and plane.

In using more sport-specific exercises and methods, specificity in strength training becomes dominant as the athlete approaches the stage of high performance. So the instructor has to select the type of equipment that best suits the needs of the sport. Although you can use some machines in certain training phases (i.e., maximum strength phase), free weights seem to be more practical. They have a greater mechanical similarity to most athletic skills and coordinate different muscle groups. Although a proper technique is more difficult to learn, free weights allow the athlete to perform moves in various directions and planes. The athlete can duplicate most of the dynamic nature of sport actions to create a sport-specific acceleration throughout the range of motion. In fact, this is one of the most important advantages of free weights.

Free weights are popular but can cause injury if improperly used. Besides teaching the technique, the instructor should ensure that a spotter is constantly assisting the performer. The main objective of spotting is safety and injury prevention.

As the instructor introduces a new movement, he or she should do the following:

- Explain the main elements of lifting.
- Demonstrate the correct technique.
- Have the athlete perform the movement with low load and remark on execution.
- Explain and demonstrate the role of the spotter.

An effective spotter, usually one of the instructors or an experienced athlete, should do the following:

- Know the technique of lifting as well as the appropriate spotting technique.
- Give the performer the necessary technical clues.
- Throughout the performance, know the program (number of repetitions) in order to be attentive and effective in his or her role.

The methodology of developing strength changes and becomes more difficult as the athlete approaches maturation. The athlete is now seeking to train for maximum strength or one of its components, power or muscular endurance, not only to develop general strength.

Training Program

Postpuberty includes young people from the ages of 13 and 14 up to 18, or the beginning of maturation. Because there are so many biological and psychological differences among young people in this age range, I have decided to divide the training program into two parts: early and late postpuberty.

Training Program for Early PostPuberty

Because the biological and psychological potentials of early postpuberty children (approximately 14 to 15 years old) are closer to puberty than adulthood, a training program can still use circuit training with great benefit for continuous athletic improvement. The great difference between a circuit-training program for puberty and early postpuberty lies in the following:

- Exercises are more difficult.
- Load for some exercises will be higher.
- Rest interval between exercises will be lower.

Two examples of circuit training are presented here (tables 6.4 and 6.5). The second one is more difficult and has more power exercises such as plyometrics.

Use the suggested load and number of repetitions flexibly. For some they might be too difficult, for other young athletes too easy. Therefore, please adjust the program to individual potentials.

Table 6.4	Circuit Training for Early Postpuberty	
Exercises	**Number of reps/duration in sec**	**Rest interval (sec)**
• Pull-up	4 - 8	30
• Leg press 50kg/110lb	10 - 12	30
• Trunk twist	8 - 10	30
• Lats pull down 40kg/88lb	6 - 8	30
• Slalom jump	30 sec	60
• Arm curl 40kg/88lb	6 - 8 (10)	30
• MB trunk raise	6 - 8	60
• Push-up	6 - 8 (10)	30
• Cone jump	30 sec	120

Note: Do two circuits. Adjust weights as per children's potential.

Table 6.5	Circuit Training for Early Postpuberty (More Challenging)		
Exercises	Load	Number of reps/duration in sec	Rest interval (sec)
• Leg press	60kg/132lb	12 - 15	20
• Pull-up	—	4 - 6	30
• V-sit	—	4 - 6 (8)	30
• Vertical hop	—	30 sec	30
• Chest press	40kg/88lb	6 - 8	20
• Trunk extension	—	6 - 8 (10)	20
• Scissors splits	—	30 sec	30
• Lats pull down	40kg/88lb	6 - 8 (10)	20
• Cone jump	—	30 sec	120

Note: Do two circuits. Apply program as per individual potential.

Training Program for Late PostPuberty

Late post-puberty includes athletes approximately 16 to 17 years old. Assuming that strength training follows technical work, it is a complementary activity that can have a duration of 30 to 60 minutes, especially during the competitive phase. You can change this trend during some segments of the preparatory phase by organizing a strength-training session apart from technical or tactical training. In either case, the instructor should make sure that the athletes have a comprehensive warm-up.

Table 6.6 refers to an annual plan in which the competitive phase is during the summer months. Based on this model, you can create a different plan in which the competitions are either in the fall (i.e., football) or winter (i.e., skiing, basketball, etc.). You can easily apply table 6.6 to an endurance sport in which the volume would be high but the intensity (load) low to medium. Please note that below the training phases I have indicated the periodization of strength or the type of strength to be training in that phase.

Training Program for Each Type of Strength

I suggest here a training program for each type of strength—maximum strength (see table 6.7) and power development (see table 6.8). Anatomical adaptation is the only exception here, for which you can organize a circuit training as mentioned earlier.

Please adjust the program according to your environment, the equipment available to you, and, most important, the abilities and backgrounds of your athletes. For athletes reaching maturity (18 years or more) in college athletics, or professional athletes, I suggest you consider another book of mine, *Periodization of Training for Sports*, published by Human Kinetics in 1999.

As parents or instructors may organize their own programs, I ask that you please consider the following important points:

- Do not use loads over 80 percent of 1RM. Your athlete may not be ready for it.
- Alternate per week workouts for maximum strength and power.
- In any program try to have two exercises for both arms and legs.
- Athletes must perform power exercises dynamically and explosively.
- Do not shorten the rest interval. If anything, increase it!
- Do not push! Your athlete still has a few years ahead of him or her before using heavy loads (over 80 percent) or taxing workouts.

A training log is always convenient for keeping records of your athlete's training and monitoring his or her progress more efficiently. Please refer to the training log in table 6.9.

| Table 6.6 | **Periodization Model for Strength Training for Annual Plan for Late Postpuberty** |

Dates	Nov	Dec	Jan	Feb	Mar	Apr	May	Jun	Jul	Aug	Sep	Oct
Training phase	Preparatory						Competitive				Transition	
Periodization of strength	AA			- M × S < 80% - Power			Power				AA	

Notes: AA = Anatomical adaptation.

MxS = Maximum strength with a load below 80% of 1RM.

| Table 6.7 | **Strength-Training Program for Maximum Strength (<80%)** |

Exercises	Load % 1RM	Number of reps	Number of sets	Rest interval (sec)
• Leg press	70 - 80%	6 - 8	2	2
• Chest press	70%	8	2	2
• Abdominal arch	—	8 - 10 (12)	1	1
• Trunk extension	—	12 - 15	1	1
• Half squat	60 - 70%	10 - 12	2	2
• Drop push-up	—	6 - 10	1	1
• Leg curl	50%	8	2	3
• Pull-up	—	Maximum	2	2
• Inclined overhead leg lift	—	8 - 10	1	2

Note: — means no load or own body weight.

Table 6.8   Strength-Training Program for Power Development

Exercises	Number of reps	Number of sets	Rest interval (min)
• Wall push-up	8 - 10 (12)	2	2
• Knee-tuck jump	15 - 20	2	2
• Abdominal thrust	8 - 10	1	1
• Trunk extension	6 - 10	1	2
• MB chest throw	15 - 20	2	2
• Double-leg burpee	8-10	2	2

Table 6.9   Training Log

	Exercises	Sets					
		1	2	3	4	5	6

Enter exercise load and number of repetitions per set (example 180 × 6).

Exercises for Prepuberty

From the multitude of exercises for strength training, the following exercises are guidelines only and not restrictions. You can use other exercises, depending on the environment and facilities.

DUMBBELL SIDE RAISE

Area worked: shoulders

1. Begin standing, feet apart, arms at the side.

2. Lift the arms up above the head.

3. Return to starting position.

DUMBBELL CURL

Area worked: biceps

1. Begin standing, arms extended down in front of the hips, palms facing upward.

2. Flex right elbow, lifting weight toward right shoulder.

3. Return to starting position. Repeat with the left arm.

DUMBBELL SHOULDER PRESS

Area worked: shoulders, especially trapezius

1. Begin standing, holding the dumbbells at shoulder level.

2. Press dumbbells straight above the shoulders.

3. Return them to starting position.

DUMBBELL OVERHEAD RAISE

Area worked: shoulders

1. Lie on your back, arms along the body.

2. Raise both arms up and over the head to the floor.

3. Return to the starting position.

Variation

Repeat the same with each arm alternately.

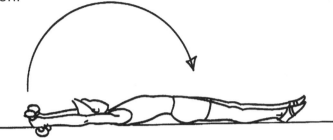

DUMBBELL FLY

Area worked: chest and shoulders

1. Lie on your back, arms extended to the sides.

2. Raise both arms to vertical (above the chest).

3. Return to starting position.

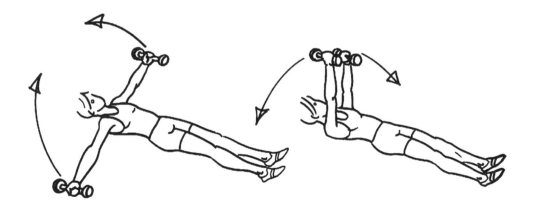

Athletes perform most medicine ball exercises with catching and throwing. The thrower performs the action progressively faster, achieving maximum acceleration at the end. The catcher anticipates the ball by extending the arms forward to receive it. As the athlete catches the medicine ball, the arms flex progressively to absorb the shock. After absorbing the shock, the athlete can maintain momentum, and by performing a semicircular motion, the speed of the ball accelerates, culminating in another throw.

Note: Suggested weight for the medicine ball is 2 kilograms (4 pounds) for prepuberty, 3 to 4 kilograms (7 to 9 pounds) for puberty, and 4 to 6 kilograms (9 to 13 pounds) for postpuberty.

MEDICINE BALL CHEST THROW

Area worked: shoulders and arm extensors (triceps)

1. Begin standing, two partners facing each other, 8 to 10 feet apart, with partner A holding a medicine ball in front of the chest.

2. Partner A extends the arms up and forward, throwing the ball toward the chest of partner B.

3. After catching the ball, partner B throws the ball back to partner A.

MEDICINE BALL TWIST THROW

Area worked: arms, trunk, and oblique abdominal muscles

1. Partner A faces partner B with his or her left side, holding the ball at hip level.

2. Partner B faces partner A anticipating the ball with arms extended forward.

3. Partner A turns the body to the left, arms extended, releasing the ball through the side toward partner B.

4. After catching the ball, partner B takes the same starting position (side facing partner A), performs a rotation, returning the ball to partner A in the same manner.

MEDICINE BALL FORWARD OVERHEAD THROW

Area worked: chest, shoulders, arms, and abdominal muscles

1. Partners face each other, 2.5 to 3 meters (8 to 10 feet) apart, with partner A holding the ball above the head.

2. Partner A extends the arms backward, then immediately forward toward the chest of partner B.

3. After catching the ball, partner B returns it to partner A with the same motion.

MEDICINE BALL SCOOP THROW

Area worked: ankles; knees; hip extensors; and arm, shoulder, and back muscles

1. Begin standing, feet apart, holding the ball between the legs.

2. Bend the knees, then immediately extend them, throwing the ball vertically with the arms.

3. Extend arms upward to catch the ball, and return to the starting position.

Variation

You can perform the same exercise with a partner.

ABDOMINAL CRUNCH

Area worked: abdominal and hip flexor muscles

1. Lie on the floor, arms along the body, with either a partner or furniture holding your feet on the ground. Knees are slightly bent.

2. Raise the upper body up and forward, touching the knees with the chest.

3. Relax and bring the trunk slowly back to starting position.

MEDICINE BALL BACK ROLL

Area worked: abdominals and hip flexors

1. Lie on the back, arms along the body, holding a medicine ball between your feet, with knees slightly bent.

2. Raise the legs above the head.

3. Lower legs back to starting position.

Variation

You can perform the same exercise with a partner, throwing the ball backward overhead.

Note: When the ball is above your face, place your palms over your face to catch it so it doesn't fall on your face or head.

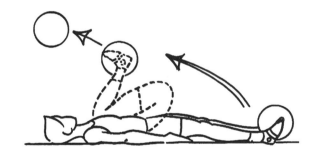

TRUNK TWIST

Area worked: abdominal obliques

1. Sit with a partner holding your feet or resting them under a heavy object or stall bars; hands are behind your neck, knees slightly bent.

2. Lean slightly back, with the trunk in an oblique position. Turn the trunk to the left as far as possible.

3. Return to the starting position, and turn the trunk to the right as far back as possible.

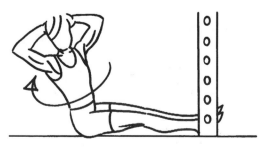

119

SINGLE-LEG BACK RAISE

Area worked: hip extensors and spine muscles

1. Lie on stomach, arms extended forward.

2. Lift left leg upward as high as possible.

3. Lower the left leg to the floor and lift the right leg.

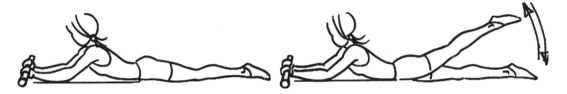

CHEST RAISE AND CLAP

Area worked: lower back muscles

1. Lie on stomach, arms extended forward on the floor.

2. Raise the chest with arms extended and perform two or three claps.

3. Relax trunk and lower arms to the floor.

SEATED BACK EXTENSION

Area worked: back and shoulder muscles

1. Sit, feet apart, two partners facing each other, arms extended in front of the shoulders, hands firmly grasped.

2. Partner B performs an upper-body extension and partner A resists it slightly, so partner B can perform the motion slowly.

3. Repeat with partners changing roles.

TWO-LEG SKIP

Area worked: calf and knee extensor muscles

1. Two children hold the ends of a skipping rope, with the third ready to skip the rope.

2. Rope holders rotate the rope, while the performer jumps up and down to avoid being hit by the rope.

3. Stop the action after 15 to 20 seconds, and change roles.

Variations

• One-leg skip on the spot.

• Two-leg forward skips.

• One-leg skip forward.

• Two-leg backward skips.

• One-leg backward skips.

• Alternate one- and two-leg skips forward and backward.

LOOP SKIP

Area worked: calf and knee extensors

1. Two teams are lined up behind a starting line. Each team has a cone 15 meters or yards in front of them.

2. At the signal, players skip the rope while moving forward, loop around the cone, and return to starting position.

3. The rope goes to the next player, and the first performer goes to the end of the line.

4. Each player skips the rope as fast as possible.

5. The winning team is the one having all players skipping over the course and finish line first.

Variation

Time individual performance (going over the course from start to finish).

121

DODGE THE ROPE

Area worked: calf and knee extensors

1. A group of players form a circle. In the middle of the circle there is a player holding the end of a skipping rope. The distance from the player in the middle to the circle is equal to the length of the rope.

2. The player in the middle swings the rope in a circle at ankle height. As the rope approaches each player, he or she jumps over it.

3. When the rope hits a player, he or she goes in the middle of the circle.

ZIGZAG MEDICINE BALL THROW

Area worked: arms and shoulders

1. Two equal teams line up where they can throw a ball in zigzag: 4 meters (10 feet) aside and in front of each other. The first player holds a medicine ball.

2. Throw the ball with two hands, from player to player.

3. The first team that completes the course is the winner.

Variation

Throw the ball with one hand, overhead with two arms, and from the side.

MEDICINE BALL SIDE PASS RELAY

Area worked: abdominal obliques and shoulders (deltoids)

1. Two equal teams sit with their feet apart.

2. The first player holds the ball.

3. Calculate the distance between players so they can perform the pass comfortably.

4. The first player rotates to the right, passing the ball to the next player.

5. Continue this as fast as possible to the end of the line.

6. The last player stands up, runs to the front as quickly as possible, sits down, and starts the series again.

7. The relay is over when the first player is at the end of the row.

8. The winner is the team that finishes first.

Variations

• Pass the ball alternately to each side.

• Pass the ball back over the head.

• Hold the ball between your feet, roll over, and pass the ball to the feet of the next player.

Exercises for Puberty

Exercises for puberty allow benefits such as developing coordination and agility, but in a form of play or games in which the children perform a basic strength exercise. The variety of movements children perform help them develop basic coordination and agility and awareness of how muscles work in different positions.

SINGLE-LEG BURPEE

Area worked: shoulders and back muscles

1. Push-up stand, right leg bent under the chest, the left leg extended backward.

2. Exchange leg positions by bringing the left leg to the starting position, right leg backward.

3. Repeat same to fatigue.

Variation

Double-leg burpee

PUSH-UP

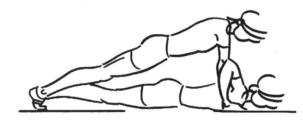

Area worked: shoulders, triceps, and back muscles

1. Push-up stand, elbows extended.

2. Bend elbows to lower body to floor level.

3. Return to starting position.

CLAP PUSH-UP

Area worked: shoulders, triceps, wrist extensors, and back muscles

1. Push-up stand, elbows extended.

2. Bend elbows to lower body to floor level, and extend the elbows vigorously above the floor.

3. At the highest level, push the palms against the floor and quickly perform a clap.

4. As the body descends toward the floor, place the palms again on the floor and push up aggressively to continue the exercise.

5. After you perform the desired number of repetitions, return to starting position.

BACKWARD OVERHEAD SHOT THROW

Area worked: hip and knee extensors, back, and shoulder muscles

1. Stand, feet apart, hands holding the shot between the legs.

2. Extend knees, hips, and upper body, and by swinging the arms backward, throw the shot backward overhead.

3. Bring arms relaxed along the body, take a shot, and repeat.

MEDICINE BALL SIDE THROW

Area worked: abdominal obliques, leg extensors, and shoulder muscles

1. Partner A holds the medicine ball on right side of the hips, back facing partner A.

2. Partner A rotates the trunk, hips, and shoulders dynamically, throwing the ball toward partner B.

3. Partner B catches the ball, turns to face partner A with his or her back, and repeats same.

FORWARD SHOT/MEDICINE BALL THROW

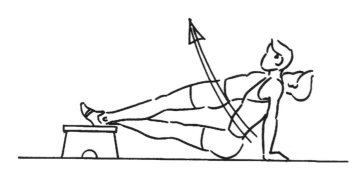

Area worked: leg extensors, hips, back, and arm and shoulder muscles

1. Stand facing direction of throw, hips and knees flexed. Feet at shoulder width, shot/medicine ball held on both palms, arms fully extended.

2. Swing the arms back between the legs. Swing the upper body and arms forward, extending the knees and hips, and release the shot/medicine ball forward.

3. Fetch the shot and perform same again.

Variation

Perform same with a partner 4 meters (15 feet) apart.

HIP THRUST

Area worked: abdominals, hip flexors, and arm and shoulder muscles

1. Sit, feet rested up on a bench or any high object (one foot above ground), hands on the ground, slightly behind the hips.

2. Thrust the hips upward to horizontal (or higher), in full body extension.

3. Relax and lower hips to starting position.

HANG HIP FLEXION

Area worked: abdominals, hip flexors, and finger flexor muscles

1. Hold body hanging straight down by gripping with the hands on a high bar, rings, or something similar.

2. Lift both knees up, toward the stomach.

3. Relax and return legs to starting position.

Variations

• One leg at a time.

• Lift legs with knees straight.

MEDICINE BALL SIT-UP THROW

Area worked: abdominal and shoulder muscles

1. Partner A stands, feet apart, holding the ball. Partner B sits, feet apart, knees slightly flexed.

2. Partner A tosses the medicine ball toward the chest of partner B. As partner B catches the ball, he or she rocks back toward the floor, then, using the momentum of an upper-body forward thrust, throws the ball back to partner A.

3. Return to starting position. Alternate roles.

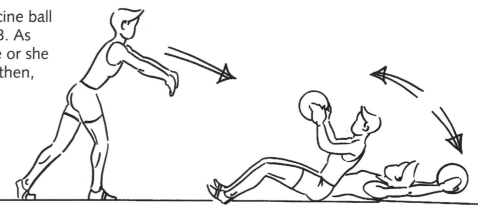

BETWEEN-LEG MEDICINE BALL BACKWARD THROW

Area worked: abdominal and shoulder muscles

1. Partner A stands, feet apart, holding a medicine ball above head. Partner B faces the back of partner A.

2. Flex hips dynamically, bringing hands between legs, releasing the medicine ball backward toward partner B.

3. Partner B catches the ball, turns around, and performs same toward partner A.

DOUBLE-LEG SIDE LIFT

Area worked: oblique abdominal muscles

1. Partner A stands, feet apart, while partner B lies down, head near partner A's feet, and grasps the ankles of partner A.

2. Partner B lifts the legs up to vertical, lowering them to the floor, up again to vertical, and down again to the other side.

3. Return legs to starting position. Alternate roles.

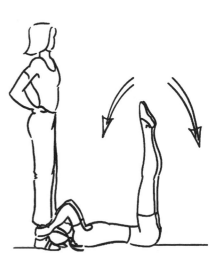

MEDICINE BALL TRUNK RAISE

Area worked: back, hips, and shoulder muscles

1. Partner A is lying on his or her stomach, holding the ball above the head. Partner B supports A's ankles.

2. Partner A raises the ball by arching the back.

3. Return to starting position.

4. Each partner performs alternately.

TRUNK RAISED MEDICINE BALL THROW

Area worked: back and shoulder muscles

1. Lying on their stomachs, head to head, 3 meters (10 feet) apart, partner A grasps the ball that rests on the floor.

2. Partner A arches the body back, lifting the ball, then throws it to B.

3. Partner B catches it and throws it back to A.

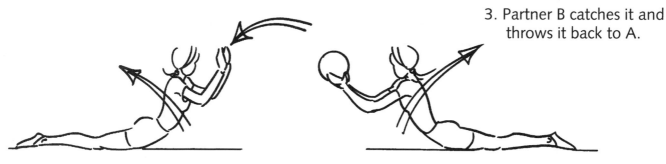

OVERHEAD MEDICINE BALL BACKWARD THROW

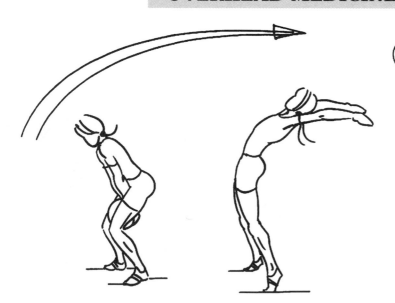

Area worked: back and shoulder muscles

1. Begin standing, feet apart, holding medicine ball between your legs.

2. Swing arms up and backward, arch body, and throw the ball backward.

3. Fetch the ball and do the same again.

Variation

Perform the movement with a partner.

MEDICINE BALL CHEST PASS RELAY

Area worked: arm strength; leg strength; acceleration

1. Two or more teams line up facing their captain.

2. He or she passes the ball to the first player who passes it back, goes to the end of the line, and sits down.

3. The team that finishes first and sits down quickly is the winner.

OVER-UNDER BRIDGE RELAY

Area worked: knee extensors, abdominals, and trunk extensors

1. Teams pass the medicine ball alternately over the head and between the legs.

2. The last player runs quickly with the ball to the front of the line and starts again.

3. The team that finishes first is the winner.

129

ROLL MEDICINE BALL UNDER THE BRIDGE

Area worked: shoulders and legs (sprinting)

1. Teams stand in line, feet part. The first player rolls the ball between the legs to the last player in line, then moves to the back of the line.

2. The last player catches the ball and runs quickly in front to continue the task.

3. The team that finishes first is the winner.

Variation

Roll the ball with two hands.

OBSTACLE RUN RELAY

Area worked: balance, leg power (sprinting)

1. Create an obstacle course from the equipment and objects you have available.

2. Mark the course so each player has to perform the same task.

3. Time each athlete's performance to check individual improvement.

Variation

Make a competition between equal teams and calculate their total time.

BASEBALL OR TENNIS DART GAME

Area worked: shoulder strength and accuracy in throwing

1. Draw five circles on a wall. The inner circle is 30 centimeters (one foot) in diameter, and subsequent circles are 20 centimeters (eight inches) apart. The value for each circle should be 10 to 6, meaning if the athlete hits the inner circle he receives 10 points, the next circles are worth 9, 8, and 7 points, and the outer circle is worth 6 points. Draw lines at 15 meters (50 feet), 20 meters (65 feet), and 30 meters (100 feet).

2. Athletes have three throws from each distance, using overhand technique (like javelin throw or pitching).

3. Every time the ball hits an area, the athlete receives the specified score.

4. The sum of all throws represents the final score for each athlete, and all are ranked at the end of the game.

5. You could do the same with athletes in teams.

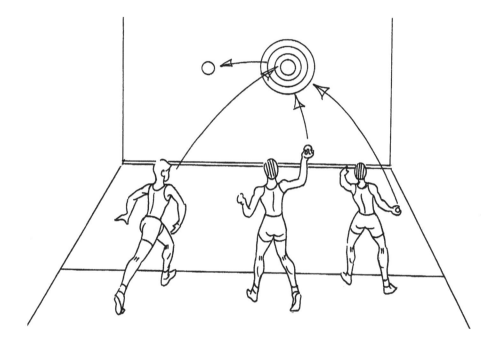

Exercises for Early Postpuberty

Most of the suggested exercises don't require a lot of equipment, and therefore can be performed at home or in a health club.

PUSH-UP PROGRESSION

Area worked: shoulders and elbow extensor muscles/triceps and trapezius

1. Push-ups against the wall (feet away and push vigorously against the wall to bring body to vertical).

2. Inclined palms supported on a chair or box.

3. Push-ups on the ground (knees).

4. Regular push-ups.

5. Clap push-ups.

6. Inclined, feet on a chair or box and hands on ground.

7. Clap push-ups from the same position as 6.

CHEST PRESS

Area worked: triceps (elbow extensors), shoulders, and chest

1. Lying on the back, grasp the handle of a universal gym, barbell, or any other chest press machine. Bend knees, place them on a bench or on the floor.

2. Press the handle up.

3. Lower the handle slowly to the starting position.

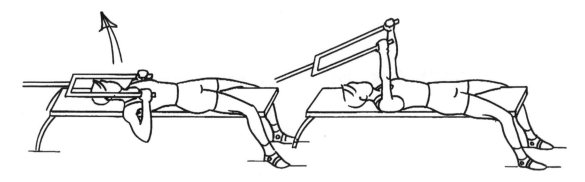

CABLE TRICEPS (ELBOW) EXTENSION

Area worked: elbow extensors (triceps) muscle

1. Stand, feet apart facing the machine. Grasp the bar, palms down, elbows bent, hands at chest height.

2. Press the handle down to hip height.

3. Return slowly and with control to starting position.

SHOULDER PRESS

Area worked: shoulder and elbow extensor muscles (trapezius and triceps)

1. Sit, with your hands palm up, placed on the handle.

2. Press handle vertically.

3. Return slowly to starting position.

LATS PULL DOWN (FRONT)

Area worked: arm flexors and lats (latissimus dorsi) muscles

1. Kneel, facing the machine, grasping the handle.

2. Pull down the handle in front to chest level.

3. Return to starting position.

ARM CURL

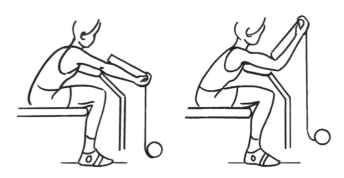

Area worked: elbow flexors (mostly biceps) muscles

1. Sit, arms extended, elbows resting on the pad. Place hands, palms up, on the small pad or handle.

2. Bend elbows to bring pad or handle to chest level.

3. Return to starting position.

INCLINE BENCH SIT-UP

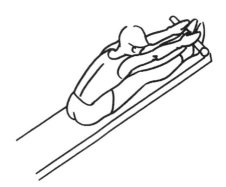

Area worked: abdominals

1. Lie on the bench, knees bent and feet supported behind the pad, arms above the head.

2. Raise upper body to touch the feet with the hands.

3. Return to starting position.

V-SIT

Area worked: abdominal and hip flexor muscles

1. Lie on floor, arms extended over the head.

2. Bring arms and legs up into a **V**-sit.

3. Return to starting position.

ABDOMINAL RAINBOW

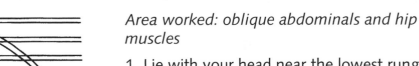

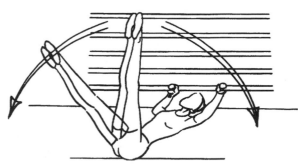

Area worked: oblique abdominals and hip muscles

1. Lie with your head near the lowest rung of a stall bar, hands gripping it.

2. Lift legs up and lower them to the right side. Lift them on the other side.

3. Rest legs on floor.

LEG PRESS

Area worked: knee extensors (quadriceps muscles)

1. Sit on a leg press chair, place the balls of your feet on the paddle.

2. Press the paddle to full leg extension.

3. Return to starting position.

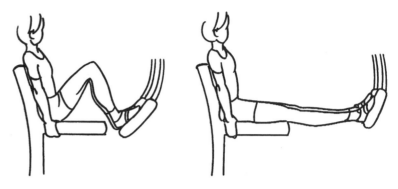

REVERSE LEG PRESS

Area worked: knee extensors and buttock muscles

1. On a leg press machine, facing away from the machine, place the ball of a foot on the paddle, the other on the floor, and hands on the T of the back support.

2. Push the paddle backward to a full extension.

3. Return to starting position and alternate legs.

LEG CURL

Area worked: knee extensors (hamstrings) muscles

1. Lie on the stomach, place heels under the top padded roller, extend knees.

2. Flex (bend) the knees, bringing pad as to close to buttocks as possible.

3. Return to starting position.

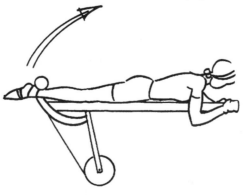
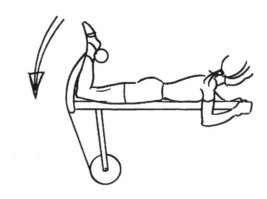

135

HALF SQUAT

Area worked: knee and hip extensors

1. Place shoulders squarely under the pads, hands grasping the bar. Place feet at shoulder width, knees bent, with the back straight.

2. Leading with head and shoulders upward, fully extend leg.

3. Return to starting position.

SLALOM JUMP

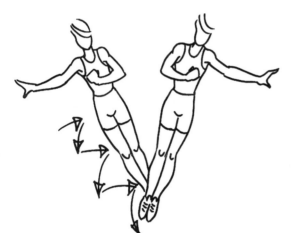

Area worked: calf and knee extensor muscles

1. Begin standing.

2. Use two feet to make continuous diagonal jumps, progressing forward in slalom fashion.

SCISSORS SPLITS

Area worked: calf and knee extensors

1. Stand, with one leg forward, the other behind.

2. Take off for a vertical jump and switch legs quickly in midair. Land and immediately jump again for continuous jumps.

VERTICAL HOP

Area worked: calf and knee extensors

1. Begin standing.

2. Swing the arms upward and press actively against the ground for a vertical spring.

3. Land, absorbing the shock, lowering the arms to hip level.

4. Repeat.

CONE JUMP

Area worked: calf, knee, and hip extensors

1. Begin standing in front of a row of cones two meters or yards apart.

2. Run and jump over each cone.

3. Return to the starting line.

CONTINUOUS SQUAT JUMP

Area worked: calf, knee, and hip extensors

1. Stand, feet apart, hands behind the head.

2. Use active upward-forward movements. Land on toes, lower heels, and slightly bend the knees to absorb the shock.

3. Repeat the sequence.

BASEBALL OR TENNIS BALL THROW FOR ACCURACY

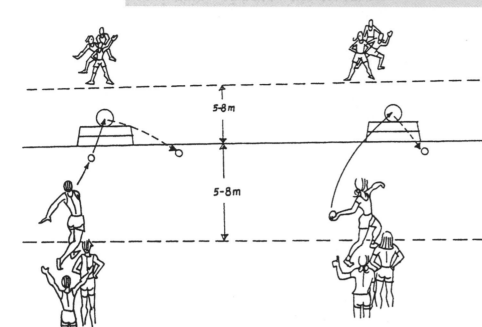

Area worked: shoulders

1. Two teams start, 10 to 15 meters or yards apart, on two lines.

2. In the middle of a gym or marked field, place two balls, bowling pins or upside-down cones so they fall easily when hit by a ball.

3. Each team or individual scores points for knocking over the cone.

Exercises for Late Postpuberty

The training program and exercises for late postpuberty are closer to the programs for high performance than those of early postpuberty. The exercises in this section are most sport-specific. In addition to the following exercises, you should also use some exercises from early postpuberty during this stage of athletic development, such as chest press (bench press), cable triceps extension, shoulder press, lats pull downs, and arm curls.

SEATED PULL-UP

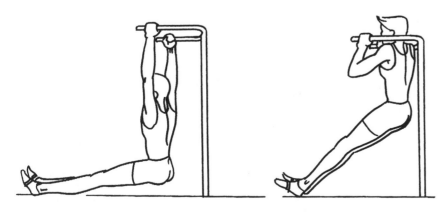

Area worked: elbow flexors, chest, and lats

1. Grasp the handles or bar with feet resting on a bench or low box.

2. Pull up the body by flexing the arms.

3. Extend arms to return to starting position.

PULL-UP

Area worked: elbow flexors, chest, and lats

1. Grasp handles or bar, arms and body extended down, palms inward.

2. Pull up the body by flexing the arms.

3. Extend arms to return to starting position.

Variation

Grasp the handle, palms facing away.

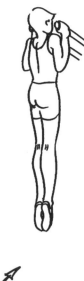

ROPE CLIMB

Area worked: wrists, arms, and shoulder flexors

1. Using arms and legs

2. Using just the arms

3. Legs at horizontal

4. One hand for each rope

5. Same, holding a medicine ball between legs

CATERPILLAR PUSH-UP

Area worked: hands, elbow extensors, shoulders, and back muscles

1. Bend hips, feet far apart, legs extended, hands at shoulder-width.

2. Bend elbows, lower shoulders toward the floor. Drive forward raising the head and extend arms straight.

3. Bring the feet close to the hands (as in the starting position) and repeat.

DIPPING

Area worked: elbow extensors and chest

1. Grasp the handles of the machine, palms in.

2. Bend elbow, lower chest toward the bar.

3. Return to starting position.

WALL PUSH-UP

Area worked: elbow extensors, chest, and shoulders

1. Partner A stands about 1 meter (2 or 3 feet) away from the wall, with partner B having palms on the upper back, and one leg placed behind the performer.

2. Partner B pushes partner A toward the wall. Partner A bends the elbows slightly to absorb the shock

3. Immediately, in a dynamic action, partner A pushes against the wall to return to starting position. Continue the action without stopping for several push-ups.

DROP PUSH-UP

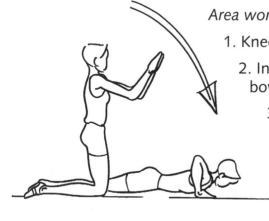

Area worked: arms flexors and extensors, chest, and back muscles

1. Kneel, with elbows bent at 90 degrees.

2. In a free fall, drop your body toward the floor, keeping elbows at 90 degrees.

3. Perform a dynamic push-up to return to starting position.

ABDOMINAL THRUST

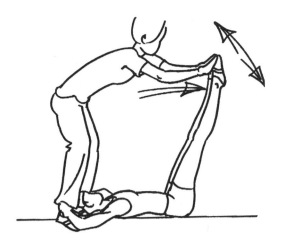

Area worked: abdominals and obliques

1. Partner A lies on back with legs on the floor, holding partner B's ankles.

2. Partner A lifts legs toward the chest of partner B. Partner B pushes the legs down, or toward one side for a series of abdominal thrusts. This creates high tension at the abdominal level.

3. Lower legs to return to starting position. Alternate roles.

ABDOMINAL ARCH

Area worked: abdominals, hips, shoulders, and back

1. Sit with your back against the stall bards, arms above head, grasping the nearest rung.

2. Press the hips actively upward, arching the body (feet are on the ground, hands firmly gripping the rung).

3. Lower hips to starting position.

INCLINED OVERHEAD LEG LIFT

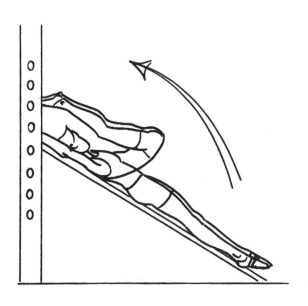

Area worked: abdominals

1. Lie on inclined bench holding a stall bar rung above the head.

2. Quickly lift the legs over the head.

3. Slowly return legs to starting position.

DOUBLE-LEG MEDICINE BALL FORWARD TOSS

Area worked: leg extensors and abdominal muscles

1. Two partners stand three meters (10 feet) apart facing each other. Partner A grasps a medicine ball between the feet and toes (toes are slightly under the ball).

2. Partner A performs a two-foot takeoff. At the approach to the highest point of the jump, slightly arch the hips, bringing the feet backward. As quickly as possible by forcefully contracting the abdominal muscles, bring the legs forward, releasing the ball toward the chest of partner B.

3. Partner B catches the ball and performs the same action.

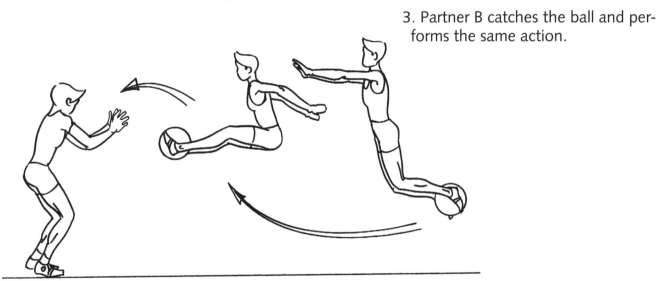

TRUNK EXTENSION

Area worked: back muscles

1. Lie on stomach on a diagonal bench, head down.

2. Arch upper body as high as possible.

3. Return to starting position and repeat.

THRUST LEGS UPWARD

Area worked: back and hip extensors

1. Lie on stomach, hips resting on a pad, arms holding a handle.

2. Thrust legs upward.

3. Lower legs to starting position and repeat.

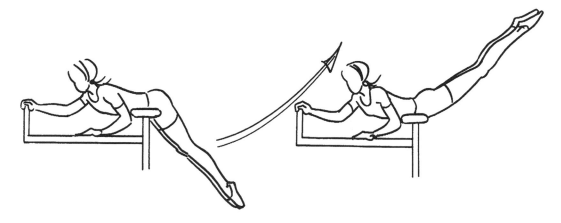

This section will focus mostly on exercises for leg power, which is often not well represented in athletic training. For leg strength, the instructor can also use exercises suggested for early postpuberty.

KNEE-TUCK JUMP

Area worked: calves, knees, and hip extensors

1. Begin standing.

2. Swing arms upward, actively pressing the feet against the ground for a vertical tuck jump.

3. Land on toes of both feet, lower arms; immediately drive arms up and spring upward again.

4. Land by flexing the knees to absorb shock and stop the jumps.

BACK KICK

Area worked: calves, knees, hip extensors

1. Begin standing.

2. Vertical jump bringing the heels to the buttocks.

3. Land on toes to absorb the shock; either continue or stop the jumps.

FORWARD ROLL AND VERTICAL JUMP

Area worked: calves, knees, hip extensors, and shoulders and arms

1. Low crouch, hands flexed at knee level.

2. Tuck the head under and roll over to a half-squat position, actively extend the legs to perform a vertical jump.

3. Land and repeat.

BACK ROLL INTO HANDSTAND

Area worked: arms and shoulders

1. Sit with chest above knees.

2. Swing the upper body backward, roll the shoulders over, palms on the ground below shoulders.

3. When approaching vertical, extend the arms into a handstand.

4. Lower legs into a low crouch, then repeat.

BACK ROLL INTO VERTICAL JUMP

Area worked: arms, shoulders, calves, knees, and hip extensors

1. Half squat.

2. Fully flex the knees, and roll backward into a full squat position. At that instant, perform an active vertical jump.

3. Land, then repeat the movement.

ROPE PUSH-UP

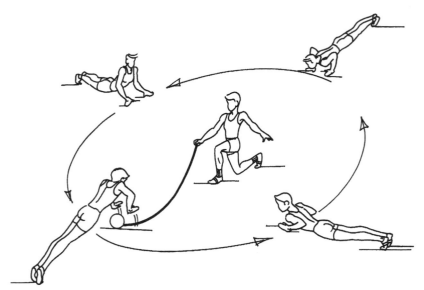

Area worked: elbow extensors, shoulders, and lower back

1. Same as previous exercise, except players perform a push-up to avoid being hit by the ball.

Please refer to "Dodge the Rope" (p. 123)

OBSTACLE RELAY

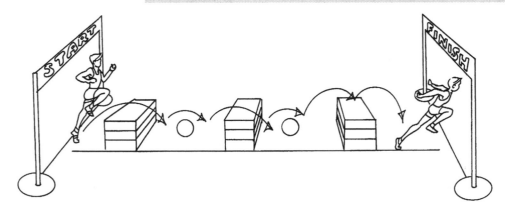

Area worked: ankle, knee, and hips extensors

1. Create an obstacle course of boxes, cones, or balls to jump over, with a short space between to run.

2. Time each athlete from start to finish.

3. Classify athletes individually or as a team.

Variation

Carry a medicine ball for the first part of the course, and at the end of the first line, throw the ball back to the next starter; then continue the course to the end.

MEDICINE BALL SPEED THROW

Area worked: shoulders and elbow extensors, and back muscles

1. Organize two rows of players in pairs, facing each other 5 meters (16 feet) apart.

2. Players from the right row have the ball.

3. The aim is to determine which pair can perform the most throws in 30 seconds (or 60, 90, 120 seconds).

4. The coach will determine the throwing technique.

Note: For between the legs forward and backward throws, increase the distance to 10 to 12 meters (33 to 39 feet).

MEDICINE BALL VOLLEYBALL GAME

Aim: To find which team is faster to score 15 points in two of three games.

Rules: Two teams of three players are in each court. Follow the rules from volleyball, except that the courts are smaller, 3 by 3 meters (10 by 10 feet), and instead of serving, players throw the ball over the net into the opposite court. The player who catches the ball passes to a teammate, who passes to another. On the third pass, the player throws the ball back over the net.

Net: Set the highest point of the net (rope, band, etc.) at the average shoulder height of the players.

Referee: The coach or a player.

Note: You can mark the court by tape or a small but visible object in each corner. Do not use balls as markers as they can cause injuries if a player steps on one. You can set a time limit for a set, for example, three sets of five minutes.

Endurance Training

Endurance, the ability to sustain physical activity for long periods, is important for sports with a duration of longer than a minute. Endurance is not only an ability of long-distance runners. A good endurance background is necessary for most athletes, from basketball or soccer to triathlon. The main benefit of endurance for most sports is to withstand the strain of training and competition. Furthermore, an athlete with a good endurance base will cope with the fatigue of training, school work, and industrious lifestyle more easily than without this foundation.

In sports, fatigue is public enemy number one! Those athletes who cannot effectively cope with fatigue have a high probability of performing poorly and losing the game, race, or match. Fatigue also affects the ability to stay focused, resulting in technical and tactical mistakes and throwing or shooting inaccuracies. This explains why, toward the end of a game or match, more mistakes are visible. If you want to improve your game, you must develop your endurance capability.

Endurance is of two types: aerobic, in which the athlete always performs the activity in the presence of oxygen, and anaerobic, in which the activity is fast, dynamic, and of short duration, so the heart does not have time to pump oxygen to the working muscles to produce energy.

Anaerobic endurance is more specific to team sports, tennis, martial arts, and so on, and longer duration sports, such as cycling, swimming, triathlon, distance running, cross-country skiing, depend more on the aerobic capacity. However, most athletes need a good aerobic base before they stress the more sport-specific anaerobic endurance.

Endurance training also has a visible health benefit. Individuals involved in endurance activities have stronger hearts and lower heart rates and blood pressure. Few of these individuals experience cardiorespiratory diseases, and the incidents of death from cardiac disease are rare. Athletes performing endurance activities use more fat as a fuel; therefore, they look trimmer. Make endurance activities part of your lifestyle.

Like speed, endurance performance is strongly influenced by genetics, because the proportion of slow-twitch muscle fibers, versus fast-twitch, largely determines an athlete's endurance potential. Genetics, or the biological makeup of an individual, may affect up to 70 percent of final performance in a sport or event in which endurance is the dominant motor quality (Matsui 1983). Other factors influencing endurance performance are psychological, such as motivation, willpower, and competitiveness. However, just because an athlete is naturally gifted for endurance activities does not mean that he or she will always be the best performer. Training ethics, determination, and motivation for hard work often can overcome a lack of talent. The best example that comes to my mind is the Czech runner Emil Zatopek, who in the 1950s and 1960s won Olympic gold medals in both the 5,000- and 10,000-meter run, breaking several world records. Emil was not the most gifted athlete, but his hard work and determination made him one of the best remembered individuals in athletics. Irrespective of talent, from childhood to maturation, all athletes can improve their endurance capacity: in early childhood as much as 10 to 20 percent per year. As they reach athletic maturation, improvement may decrease to 5 to 10 percent, although Olympic-class athletes are expected to improve their endurance potential anywhere between 3 and 7 percent annually.

Performance ability in endurance-dominant sports improves constantly during childhood, from early prepuberty to postpuberty and late adolescence. Athletes reach high performance during maturation. Female athletes may peak at a slightly earlier age than their male counterparts, perhaps due to the tendency of girls to mature earlier than boys. Throughout these development phases, boys perform better overall than girls (Hughson, 1986).

Except swimming, most endurance-dominated sports such as running, cycling, triathlon, rowing, cross-country, and canoeing are not as popular among children as team sports. Yet, the medical community and fitness specialists often associate these activities with the health benefits of physical activity, therefore implying that more people should be engaged in endurance activities. Unlike team sports, children can perform endurance activities individually or in small groups, and at an individual pace so they can enjoy them. Involvement in such activities can mean the beginning of a lifetime of fitness enjoyment and health benefit. It is not mandatory to train three or four hours per day to enjoy these sports. Shorter duration of exertion can also improve endurance, especially in early childhood.

The adaptation of children's organs and systems to endurance training has many benefits. These include improving the pulmonary (lung) and cardiac (heart) functions, and increasing the number of red blood cells that transport oxygen to the working muscles. It is only in the presence of oxygen that glycogen and fatty acids burn to produce the energy necessary for endurance activities. As the athletes train, they also become more economical in using energy, which results in improved performance.

Endurance Training Model for Initiation

Prepubescence represents the beginning of long-lasting athletic activity for many. Children's skills are poor in the early years because they have low economy of locomotion and poor tolerance for heat stress.

Prepubescent children have an inferior cardiac output (the amount of blood the heart pumps in one minute), low blood oxygen carrying capacity, and a low $\dot{V}O_2$max. However, athletes score consistently better than nonathletes, which demonstrates a certain adaptation to training. I should also mention that the average prepubescent boy has greater endurance than the average girl, partly because toward the end of prepuberty, girls have about 10 to 15 percent lower $\dot{V}O_2$max. We can explain this difference mostly because $\dot{V}O_2$max relates closely to lean body mass, increased muscular system, and low body fat, which are greater in boys. On the average, boys perform 10 to 20 percent better than girls in endurance activities. Before puberty, however, $\dot{V}O_2$max improves for both boys and girls, as does their endurance performance, both of which are due to training and the size increase of their lungs, heart, and muscular system (Hughson, 1986; Roberts et al., 1987).

Lung functioning represents a strong element in the oxygen delivery system; however, because of improper breathing techniques, as lung work increases, breathing economy and the amount of air being ventilated does not increase correspondingly. In fact, children hyperventilate, meaning a high and superficial breathing, compared with adult athletes, whose breaths are longer and deeper. Respiratory frequency decreases with age. The respiratory frequency at rest for prepubescent children is around 18 to 20 breaths per minute, and by the time they reach postpubescence, it decreases by approximately three or four breaths per minute. Children's cardiovascular systems (heart, arteries, and veins) are different from adults. The heart rate, number of heart beats per minute, during both rest and activity is higher at prepubescence (about 200 to 215 beats per minute) and falls progressively during the other developmental stages. As children grow, the heart rate frequency decreases while the efficiency increases; the lungs' vital capacity increases, which is the amount of air brought into the lungs that the body can use (Hebbelinck, 1989; Shephard, 1982).

As a result of exercise, red blood cells and hemoglobin (a complex molecule in red blood cells that contains iron and enriches the capability of red blood cells to transport oxygen) increase. At the same time, this elevates the oxygen delivery and, consequently, increases the efficiency of aerobic endurance. During prepubescence, hemoglobin concentration is approximately equal for boys and girls, but the differences in endurance proficiency rely on the other factors mentioned previously.

Scope of Endurance Training

Although you must apply it carefully, the main scope of training for prepubescence is to make children progressively able to perform an increased duration of physical activity before experiencing fatigue.

You can enhance anaerobic or aerobic endurance training through different forms of activity, such as play; games; or other endurance-related sports, for example, track and field, swimming, cycling, or cross-country skiing. Similarly, you can organize drills from team sports so that a prolonged duration or several repetitions can have positive results in endurance development.

You don't have to develop endurance for prepubescence in a regimented fashion by running laps for a given distance or speed. This would in fact be a gross disservice to children. The earlier children feel pain, the faster they will be hurt, burned out, and even willing to quit sports.

Endurance activity should be part of the multilateral development at this stage of development, and often children can perform it as part of or in addition to technical training. You should organize forms of endurance-related activities that are enjoyable, fun, and interesting for children, so they can get cardiorespiratory development as well as varied and pleasant training.

Program Design

Prepubescent children seem to cope better with activities that are either short and fast or longer than two minutes and at a slow pace. Competition distances between 200 and 800 meters or yards are unsuitable for prepubescent and pubescent children. These distances should not be part of any track and field program for young athletes, because they are unable to tolerate the lactic acid buildup specific to this type of high-intensity activity. It is only in late adolescence that athletes should incorporate these distances into a competitive program. At this stage of development, children have had the time to build strong aerobic and anaerobic backgrounds, improve the power and efficiency of the cardiorespiratory systems, and, as a result, improve their lactic acid tolerance capability.

View prepubescence as the time for early anatomical adaptation of the heart, lungs, joints, and muscles to prolonged physical activity. This should be the base on which athletes build demanding aerobic and anaerobic endurance for specialization and high performance.

Training programs that boys and girls perform together (coed) ought to be carefully planned and progressively increased over at least two or three years, depending on the entry age in the sport. Organizing such programs requires carefully applying the principles of individualization, with the knowledge that children each have their own level of tolerance to work and fatigue, and a different degree of motivation.

Now is the time to introduce different forms of play and games, and to involve children in team sports with simplified rules and the least rigidity possible. In addition, to facilitate restrictions and scheduling, children should play for as long as it is fun and not stressful.

In addition to play and games, children can develop basic endurance by running on varied terrain using the least boring methods. The instructor should use his or her imagination to organize running in small groups with various tasks and games of tag. The emphasis should be not only on running, but also on performing various tasks during the course.

Children can develop basic endurance through individual activities such as swimming, boating, cycling, or cross-country skiing. However, do not make such activities into competitions, but do them because the children enjoy it.

You can use table 7.1 as a guideline to plan endurance activities for prepubescent athletes. The first form of training considers play and games, which children could perform at a fast pace for a short duration, and slower if the activity is prolonged. The number of repetitions, meaning how many games or how many

Table 7.1	Periodization Model for Endurance Training for Prepuberty			
Forms of training	Distance duration	Speed of activity	Number of reps	Rest interval (min)
Play and games	—	Medium to fast (for short play)	2 - 4	Variable
Continuous relays	40 - 200 m/yd	Medium	2 - 4	2 - 3
Unstressful aerobic activity, such as running, swimming, rowing, and cross-country skiing	20 - 60 min	Low and steady	1 - 2 (depending on the distance)	—

times children do a game in a session is two to four, with a rest interval as long as necessary so children are fully rested before starting again.

If children perform relays of longer distance, up to 200 meters or yards, the speed cannot be higher than medium. At this age children cannot run 200 meters or yards with high velocity. Children can repeat relays two to four times, always taking a break of two or three minutes before doing it again.

Children can easily perform longer duration activities, such as running, swimming, and cross-country skiing, over 20 to 60 minutes if the speed of activity is low. While performing such activities, do not push the children. Let them find their own activity speed and allow the real challenge to be the distance. It is better to have them perform an activity for a long distance at slow pace than to do a short distance and a fast pace.

Endurance Training Model for Athletic Formation

As athletes reach puberty, their endurance improves. If pubescence represents the beginning of organized training, then young athletes can expect fast improvements in endurance capacity simply because their pretraining endurance level was low.

Children can improve $\dot{V}O_2$max during puberty, with the highest gains occurring during the growth spurts. Although $\dot{V}O_2$max increased at approximately the same rate for boys and girls during prepubescence, puberty accelerates endurance gains for boys. This is mostly because of increased muscle mass in boys, whereas girls tend to gain body fat instead. As a result, boys have a higher aerobic capacity, and a larger cardiac and pulmonary capacity (Hughson, 1986; Shephard, 1982).

Most changes pubescent athletes experience are genetically determined. Some of their dramatic changes during puberty manifest in their aerobic endurance. Young athletes experience visible phases of stagnation of endurance development. At times, coaches notice a temporary plateau, or even a decline, in aerobic endurance, in spite of the continuity of training.

You can also observe temporary changes in trainability during pubescence. About half a year before a leap in growth, there can be a visible decrease in endurance training potential. Before and after a growth spurt, however, gains in endurance capacity appear at a faster rate. We can conclude, therefore, that the level exerted in endurance capacity depends on the children's changes in dimensions.

Pubescence for girls represents the stage of fastest and probably the best gains in endurance, although as already mentioned, their male counterparts accelerate faster. It is possible that girls might never reproduce the performance they reach during pubescence, unless they are participating in organized training. The main reason for performance depreciation in girls is postpubescent gains in total body fat.

The size of the heart and lungs directly affects the oxygen delivery system (cardiorespiratory). Boys' organs are better developed due to the anatomical size of the lungs and increased involvement in physical activities. The respiratory frequency at rest is approximately 18 breaths per minute for both sexes; however, compared with adults, children's respiratory pattern is more superficial and rapid. This makes children hyperventilate during exercise, which results in higher breathing frequency and lower efficiency in oxygen use. Puberty represents the stage of other gender differences as well, such as red blood cell count and hemoglobin concentration, with boys having significantly greater values due to increased physical activity.

Although heart rates during exercise decline with age, beginning with puberty and continuing to maturation, boys have slightly lower rates because of a larger and more powerful heart. At puberty the highest rates begin to fall at approximately one or two beats per year. The highest heart rate during exercise is also recorded before or during puberty, ranging from 195 to 215 beats per minute (Bailey, Malina, and Mirwald, 1985; Malina, 1984). Factors such as poor fitness levels, obesity, anxiety, and heat stress also influence heart rate, especially for untrained individuals.

During the phases of growth spurts, children may be vulnerable to muscle injuries resulting from long-distance activities, and if exaggerated the overuse syndrome may be visible. This can be even more likely when running long distances on hard surfaces. Therefore, consider the benefits of regular aerobic training against the eventual negative results. Parents and coaches should be careful in applying regimented training that may result in pain or even health risks. Long-distance activities require an extended training time, which may stop children from doing enjoyable social activities such as play and learning other skills.

Scope of Endurance Training

Any endurance training program designed for pubescent athletes should be an attempt to increase the endurance foundation for aerobic and anaerobic endurance, and to take any endurance gains made during prepuberty to a higher level.

An equally important scope is to continue developing and strengthening the cardiorespiratory system, increasing the power of the heart to pump blood to the working muscles more effectively. This will be visible through a progressive decrease in heart rate and an increase in the cardiac output or the amount of blood pumped per minute.

From puberty on there is a clear differentiation of endurance capacity between girls and boys, so training programs have to address their specific conditions.

View pubescence as the beginning of an effectively organized endurance training. Its development benefits overall fitness and buffers fatigue. The better the endurance level, the easier an athlete will cope with an increased number of training hours per week and the total demand in training, which will increase during puberty and postpuberty. Improved endurance will also result in faster recovery between training sessions, making athletes better conditioned to tolerate a progressively increasing training load.

Program Design

Endurance training for pubescence should progress toward specialization, in which training specificity becomes dominant.

As table 7.2 shows, the program can expand to include middle-distance events in track and field, and increase to longer distances, from 800 meters to 2,000 meters (.5 mile to 1.25 miles). Because running is an important activity for most sports, now is the time to teach children a correct technique for running. To accomplish this, design the program around technical acquisition, meaning that the athlete should perform the distance or the number of repetitions only as long as the skill is correct. When fatigue sets in, technique starts to fall apart, and continuing work under these conditions will be counterproductive.

Continue to develop most of the endurance program during the technical and tactical work. However, you should also consider performing endurance training apart from this work (the so-called conditioning). In such situations, the instructor must remember that each segment of training is fatiguing and should consider total fatigue when calculating the training load (including conditioning).

Consider the following steps when progressively increasing the load in endurance-related training:

1. At first, increase the duration of a training session from 45 minutes to 60, 75, and up to 90 minutes.

2. Increase the number of training sessions per week from two or three to four, five, and in some sports higher.

3. Increase the number of drills or repetitions per training session. When the duration of a session reaches the limit, and you have maximized the num-

Table 7.2	**Periodization Model for Endurance Training for Puberty**			
Forms of training	**Distance**	**Speed of activity**	**Number of reps**	**Rest interval (min)**
Play, and relays, as in prepuberty	40 - 200 m/yd	Fast to medium	3 - 5	Variable
Interval training runs	200 - 400 m/yd	Medium	3 - 5 (low numbers for 400 m/yd)	2 - 3
Aerobic activity (long repetition)	800 - 2,000 m (.5 mi to 1.25 mi)	Medium and steady, at times feel slight discomfort	1 - 3	3 - 5

ber of workouts per week, the next step is to progressively do more repetitions per training session. Now training demand is higher and endurance benefits increase.

4. Increase duration covered in each repetition. If a drill or repetition has lasted 45 seconds in the past, at this stage of load increment, you may extend the duration to 60, 70, or more seconds.

As the duration of training expands, children start perspiring more and therefore should take fluids before, during, and after training. Any parent or coach must consider frequent water breaks, especially in hot and humid conditions, so that children have a body heat balance and avoid losing too much fluid.

Training Program

A training program designed for pubescent athletes should still consider different forms of play and games, as well as elements of more formal training aimed at developing endurance. As much as possible, the coach should consider variety and enjoyment in the complexity of activities he or she is planning. Although training for endurance often means perseverance in repeating the same kind of work over and over again, avoid regimentation.

Repetition of certain types of endurance training should not necessarily mean boring laps. You can make training enjoyable by varying the distance, the terrain, and arranging a fun course. For team sports, coaches should organize the duration of technical and tactical drills with endurance development in mind. A 60-second duration drill will have not only technical or tactical merit, but also sport-specific endurance development.

An endurance training program should include different distances or durations, because they each may develop a component of endurance. For instance, an activity with a long, steady pace will develop the pumping power of the heart, the stroke volume (the amount of blood pumped per beat), and, in the long run, will decrease the resting heart rate. Some types of work, mainly aerobic training, develop the capillary network, the branching out of veins and arteries, so that oxygen will travel to every part of the body.

Interval training, which is a method of repeating a distance or time several times, with a prescribed intensity, duration, and rest interval, strengthens the heart and lungs. If the duration of work is between two and three minutes, the athlete develops $\dot{V}O_2$max. By performing shorter repetitions, the athlete will progressively adjust to anaerobic endurance. Because such a training program produces lactic acid, a fatiguing by-product of anaerobic training, you must apply it carefully and progressively. Its maximum use will be during postpuberty, and mostly during training for high performance. From this point of view, pubescence, especially the latter part, is the time to introduce interval training.

The type of interval training appropriate for puberty is mostly anatomical adaptation, rather than training for physiological improvement and performance increases. This means medium distance and time, with medium intensity, and a rest interval for a full regeneration. As a result of such a program, children should have the time (two to four years) to adjust anatomically before training physiologically. Children can achieve the anatomical adaptation phase of interval training without the typical strain of short- and high-intensity interval training, which results in a high heart rate (close to or even over 200 beats per minute). Such a heart rate has a low stroke volume and decreases the ability to effectively pump oxygen and the glucose needed for producing energy. There is a misconception that interval training is short and must hurt.

The main training law for endurance training for puberty is "Before training physiologically, train anatomically" (the anatomy of the cardiorespiratory system).

Considerations for Specialization

Endurance and endurance performance improve steadily throughout the growing years. During adolescence, you may notice a slight acceleration for males, but not as much for females. The mean $\dot{V}O_2$max remains at about the same level (Armstrong and Davies, 1984; Shephard, 1982). As athletes better adapt to training, the energy expenditure becomes more effective, more economical, and performance may constantly improve. Improved performance, therefore, relates to improved energy economy, independent of the dynamics of aerobic power.

The biological differences, as well as performance differences, continue to grow during postpuberty. In addition, females are less likely to reach their full physical potential because of social factors and not necessarily because of biological handicaps. Society is used to the fact that sport participation is dominated by males. Although many changes have occurred in societal acceptance of equal opportunities for males and females in sport participation, men's sports still have higher visibility. The lack of prominent role models, reduced interest from the media, and even the peer conduct regarding women's participation in sports all represent social and psychological constraints for many young girls. Changes in attitude should not exclude the possibility of bridging the gap between endurance performance for female and male athletes.

Scope of Endurance Training

On the foundation of endurance built during prepubescence and pubescence, training now becomes more specific to meet the needs of the selected sport.

Diversity training that I promoted in the past is progressively narrowed during this development stage, especially as the athlete approaches high performance. For endurance training, diversity means variations and combinations between aerobic and anaerobic training.

The long-term approach to endurance training pursued during prepuberty and puberty will reach a peak during postpuberty and maturation. From postpuberty on, however, the coach has to develop annual plans that include aerobic and anaerobic training, as well as introducing ergogenesis training.

Ergogenesis is a term of Greek origin. *Ergon* means work, and *genesis* refers to beginning, creation. In sport interpretation, ergogenesis means create the work to combine the elements of endurance as the specifics of the sport requires. As such, ergogenesis refers to the total contribution of anaerobic and aerobic endurance to performance, expressed in percentage. For instance, the ergogenesis of rowing is 83 percent aerobic and 17 percent anaerobic. In 800-meter running it is 51 percent aerobic and 49 percent anaerobic. In 200-meter swimming it is 70 percent aerobic and 30 percent anaerobic. In basketball it is 40 percent aerobic and 60 percent anaerobic. Consequently, in the annual plans the coach develops, he or she has to introduce phases in which ergogenesis, or the right combination between aerobic and anaerobic endurance, dominates. The result of such a program is a progressive improvement of performance.

Program Design

Because postpuberty represents the stage of specialization, when athletes start to specialize in an event, sport, and position in team sports, training specificity gets high visibility. Even under these conditions, however, you should not exclude multilateral training. The athlete must continue to work on the foundation of aerobic capacity, the ability to produce energy under aerobic conditions.

Anatomical adaptation of the cardiorespiratory system, strengthening the heart and improving the oxygen transportation system, must be a constant objective of aerobic training. A training program for postpubescence should continually develop aerobic capacity to effectively produce and efficiently consume the oxygen this system provides.

During the first two or three years of postpubescence, developing the aerobic capacity becomes the major training objective for individual sports and team sport athletes. The last part of postpubescence endurance training becomes more specialized according to the needs of the selected sport. As mentioned previously, from now on, use anaerobic endurance and ergogenesis to build a strong aerobic base.

Constantly improving aerobic capacity to the highest possible level has certain benefits:

- It develops the oxygen transport system, in which a powerful heart plays an important role.

- Athletes can prevent hyperventilating by focusing on active exhalation—filling the lungs with fresh, oxygen-rich air—by taking deep, steady breaths.

- High aerobic capacity positively influences the anaerobic capacity because it lengthens the ability to function before reaching fatigue. An athlete with a high aerobic capacity can tolerate anaerobic work, with its highly fatiguing lactic acid buildup.

- An athlete with a high aerobic capacity can recover quickly from fatiguing training sessions or after repeating work or drills. Consequently, the athlete can slightly reduce the rest interval between repetitions and can perform more work. More work is usually translated into improved performance.

A training program designed for postpubescence also has to develop the anaerobic capacity, especially during the second part of this stage. This refers to the ability of an athlete to produce energy in the absence of oxygen and to progressively tolerate the lactic acid buildup, which is the by-product of anaerobic training.

Developing aerobic or anaerobic capacity depends on the selected training method. Long-distance training methods, including long-distance uniform (steady state), alternate interval training of long repetitions, and specific racing endurance, develop aerobic capacity. Particularly for team sports, however, the instructor should remember that athletes also can develop these capacities through specific drills, especially tactical drills. Designing longer duration drills, over three minutes, improves the aerobic component, whereas drills of 30 to 60 seconds improve the anaerobic capacity.

The training methods I suggest in table 7.3 do not exhaust what is available in sports training. However, it is critical for this stage of development, especially the early postpuberty years, to constantly emphasize aerobic training, both the uniform long-distance runs and long repetitions of interval training. Please remember that a solid aerobic base developed at this age, without strain and stress, guarantees improved performance during maturation. After all, athletes reach high performance at maturation and not at early postpuberty! Pushing young athletes often burns them out, resulting in the young athletes quitting sports.

Table 7.3 suggests the duration of rest intervals. This is just a guideline. If you want to calculate the rest interval between repetitions, please use the heart rate method, as follows:

1. Take the heart rate immediately after a repetition of an activity.
2. Continue to monitor the heart rate. When it drops to 120 beats per minute, the athlete should start another repetition.

Table 7.3	Periodization Model for Endurance Training for Postpuberty			
Forms of training	Distance/ duration	Speed of activity	Number of reps	Rest interval (min)
Uniform training (long distance)	2,000 - 5,000 m/ 1.25 - 3.1 mi	Low to medium	1	—
Interval training: long repetitions	800 - 1,500 m/ 0.5 - 1 mi	Medium	2 - 4 (6)	2 - 3
Interval training: short repetitions	200 - 400 m/yd	Medium	4 - 6	3 - 5
Tactical drills (long) for team sports	2 - 5 min	Medium	3 - 6	2 - 3
Tactical drills (short) for team sports	30 - 60 sec	Fast	4 - 6 (8)	3 - 5

Exercises for Prepuberty

The following four exercises are appropriate for prepuberty athletes.

CONTROLLED SPEED POLYGON

Focus: general endurance

1. Create your own shape (or ask the athletes).

2. Maximum running time is 15 seconds in any one section.

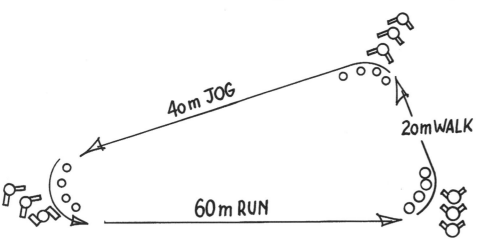

3. The class is in small groups, one at each section start point.

4. Include a variety of speed movement (e.g., jog for 40 meters or yards, run for 60 meters or yards, walk to recover for 20 meters or yards, and repeat).

SQUARE

Focus: general endurance

1. Each side is 50 meters or yards; each team begins at a corner (the corners are rounded).

2. Jog on two sides (18 to 20 seconds), walk on two sides (40 to 50 seconds).

3. Alternate walking 50 meters, jogging 50 meters, walking 50 meters, jogging 50 meters.

QUAD

Focus: general endurance

1. Divide athletes into four groups and place them at the four corners.

2. At their own pace (per group or individual child), they walk a segment, run, jog, or brisk walk.

3. They do two to four nonstop loops.

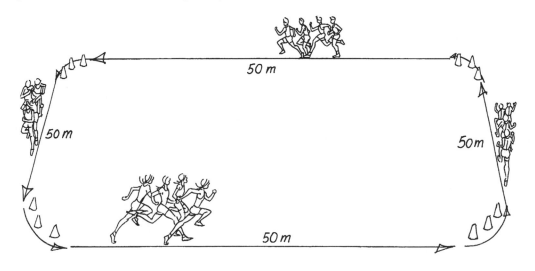

OFF INTO NATURE

Focus: general endurance

1. Mark a course of 300 to 500 meters (330 to 545 yards) in a natural setting.

2. Divide the course alternately into 100-meter (110-yard) and 50-meter (55-yard) sections using natural landmarks.

3. Walk the 50-meter (55-yard) section and jog the 100-meter (110-yard) section. Each athlete will complete the course two to four times.

Variation

For more advanced athletes, run the whole course but vary the speed of the sections.

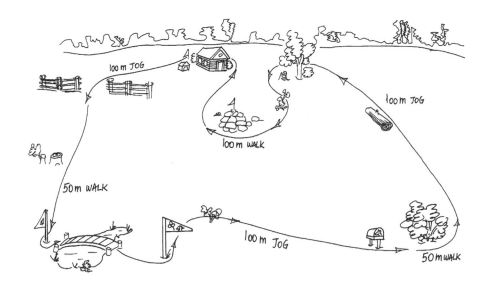

Exercises for Puberty

The following five exercises for endurance training are appropriate for puberty athletes.

AEROBIC TECHNICAL RUN

Focus: running technique

1. The technique of the distance running step has the following important elements: tall running with the head up, shoulders down and relaxed, arms swinging back and forth in coordination with the leg actions.

2. Knee drive and leg recovery are lower than in sprinting, landing on the heel and rolling over the toe for a new propulsion phase.

3. Steadiness of running and pace judgment are always important attributes for endurance running.

LONG REPETITIONS FOR PACE JUDGMENT

Focus: aerobic endurance and pace judgment

1. Run distances of 800 to 2,000 meters (1.25 miles) in a steady rhythm and even pace (pace judgment). To ensure pace judgment, the instructor can time each repetition and give feedback to the athletes, individually. However, make sure that timing the athletes is not used to create a competitive environment.

INTERVAL TRAINING RUNS

Focus: aerobic and anaerobic endurance

1. On a track, run repetitions of 200 to 400 meters at a medium and even pace.

2. Concentrate on good form, with a relaxed and steady pace.

3. Perform each repetition at the same pace.

4. Do not push yourself. Remember this is medium (60-percent) velocity.

10-MINUTE TRIANGLE RUN

Focus: aerobic endurance

1. Divide the children into three groups, each starting at the corner of the triangle.

2. Individuals can perform a combination of walk, jog, and run, according to their ability.

3. Depending on individual abilities, the same distance can be repeated 2-4 times.

4. Rest two or three minutes in the form of walking between repetitions.

Variations

• Make the triangle larger.

• Decide on a number of loops to perform for jogging, running, and walking.

• Jog for 10 minutes. Run for only 10 minutes. Increase the duration progressively to 12, 15, 20, 30 minutes, and so on.

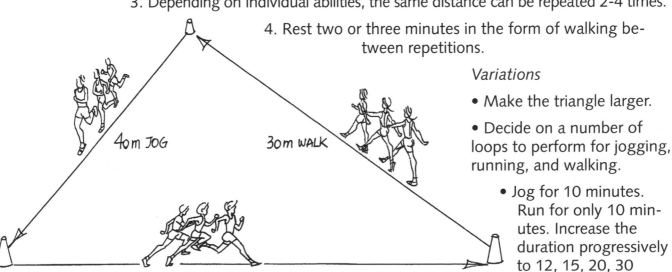

PASSING ON THE RIGHT

Focus: anaerobic and aerobic endurance

1. Teams start at marked points in an oval of a stadium and run single file.

2. Every 10 steps the last person moves to the front, passing on the right.

3. Every time the runners pass the point of the oval where they started, the instructor blows a whistle to signify the beginning of a sprint.

4. When the instructor blows the whistle again, the runners revert to the initial pace.

5. Continue this for a previously decided number of laps (i.e., 3, 4, or 5).

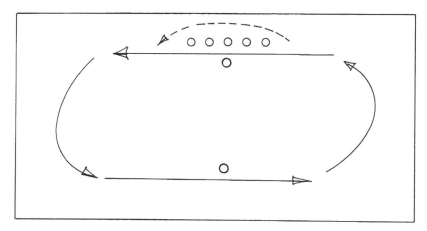

Exercises for Postpuberty

On the basis of prepuberty and puberty aerobic and anaerobic training, the scope of endurance training for postpuberty is sport specific. Athletes perform most forms of training with the implement (e.g., ball) they use in the chosen sport. Tables 7.4 and 7.5 exemplify the periodization of endurance training for postpuberty. The training program performed in the suggested phases progresses from aerobic (the months of October and November) to a mixed training, in which half of the program is interval training, to develop the anaerobic endurance, while aerobic training continues. During the competitive phase, endurance training is clearly sport specific, with at least 50 percent ergogenesis training.

During the competitive phase, the specific training for aerobic and anaerobic endurance using technical and tactical drills can follow these examples:

- Aerobic training: Specific drills of 90 seconds to 3 minutes or longer
    Rest interval of 1 or 2 minutes
    Target heart rate of 166 to 174 beats per minute
- Anaerobic training: Specific drills for 20 to 60 seconds (high-intensity drills)
    Rest interval of 2 or 3 minutes
    Target heart rate of 176 to 186 beats per minute

The coach decides the number of repetitions for each type of drill, depending on athletes' potential and the schedule of games and competitions.

Table 7.4	**Periodization for an Annual Plan for Early Postpuberty**											
Dates	Oct	Nov	Dec	Jan	Feb	Mar	Apr	May	Jun	Jul	Aug	Sep
Training phase		Preparatory								Competitive		T
Type of training		Aerobic endurance			Aerobic long intervals		Mixed aerobic and anaerobic .		Mixed specific endurance, introduce ergogenesis			Aerobic

Notes: Note the progression regarding the type of training and training content. Types of training change according to the objectives of training phases. T = Transition.

Table 7.5	**Periodization for an Annual Plan for Late Postpuberty**											
Dates	Oct	Nov	Dec	Jan	Feb	Mar	Apr	May	Jun	Jul	Aug	Sep
Training phase		Preparatory		Competitive		T	Preparatory		Competitive			T
Type of training		Aerobic	Mixed ergo.	Specific endurance ergo.		A	Aerobic	Mixed ergo.	Specific endurance ergo.			A

Note: A = Aerobic; Ergo. = Ergogenesis.

chapter 8

Excelling in Competition

Competitions represent an essential characteristic of growing and developing children in the sport environment. Properly guided competitions can benefit overall development and play an active role in children's growth and social interrelationships. Competitions give children the opportunity to apply the technical and tactical skills learned in practice to an organized game, experience winning and losing, and develop skills and values that will serve them in later life. However, there are many competitive sports programs that place excessive physical and psychological demands on children. The adverse effects of these early stresses can be detrimental to growth and may lead young participants to lose interest and drop out before fully developing their talents. Therefore, you should treat competitions only as a sporting and social tool, not as an end in itself to immediately produce a champion. A positive experience in sports and competitions can result in an active lifestyle for many years, and this is more important than being a champion athlete.

This chapter will address some controversial issues surrounding highly organized competitive sports for children and how you as a coach or parent can use competition in a positive way.

Problems With Competition

Children love to compete, but parents love it even more! In an attempt to satisfy their own thirst for competition, parents and coaches may expose children to programs that are either too aggressive or too advanced for them. Even if children are able to tolerate the physical component of the program, they may have difficulty coping mentally with the excessive emotional demands of training and competitions. Pushing children into overly demanding training and competition schedules too early, and keeping the competition-to-training ratio too large are two common ways in which coaches and parents create stress and burnout in young athletes.

Competing Too Early

Most children have their first sporting experience in organized competition. Often children as young as four years are participating in structured leagues with formal rules, referees, and official team uniforms, with winning as the primary objective.

In the United States, children of three to five years participate in competitions in swimming and gymnastics, and around five to six years in track and field, wrestling, baseball, and soccer! In other countries, for instance Brazil, children compete at six years old in soccer and swimming, and at six to eight years old in Canada, they already compete at provincial (state) level (Passer, 1988).

There are also some horror stories. In the late 1980s, a nine-year-old girl ran a marathon race in Phoenix, Arizona. A few years later, a 12-year-old girl ran a similar distance in San Francisco. Did the organizers, and especially the parents, pay any attention to medical concerns, such as excessive early training, burnout, heat injury risks, cardiac (heart) damage, reproductive changes, and impaired nutrition?

Early participation in competitions is one way in which children are pushed. From the first or second year of their training, parents or coaches enter them in important state, provincial, or national competitions. When young athletes experience demanding training and challenging competitions, this forces coaches to *artificially* push them to adapt to highly intensive work. In many cases, this approach causes children to peak at an early age, and they can indeed achieve incredible performances. The downside is that they are burned out well before they have the opportunity to excel in competitions at the proper time of physiological and psychological maturation. By this time, some have given up sports, and others who are still around rarely duplicate the performance they achieved in their midteens.

Furthermore, in sports such as track and field, children enter such events as the 400 meters (440 yards), 800 meters (880 yards), and 1,500 meters (1 mile), which are taxing events physiologically and psychologically. These events require a good training background because speed, speed endurance, anaerobic, and aerobic endurance are in high demand. Similar mistreatments occur in the triple jump. The triple jump is a series of repetitive shocks that are not absorbed by sand and the motion of bending the knees to land as in the long jump. The shocks of reactive jumps are directed straight to the spine. Children from the age of eight and up enter this event, which requires the force of takeoff and the shock of landing. In many countries in Europe, children are banned from competing in the 400 meters and the triple jump before the age of 16, when they have established enough background training.

The culprits of such mistreatments are coaches, parents, and competition organizers. To demonstrate their competency, coaches often keep win and lose records and, for some, children become just statistics! Children should not pay the price for the ambitions of coaches. Ambitious parents who want to see their children

Why Do Children Drop Out of Sports?

Michigan State University conducted the largest study ever on childhood participation in sports. This study done by Martha Ewing and Vern Seefeldt (1990), included 10,000 students. The results showed that 45 percent of 10-year-old children participate in sports. However, by age 18, the number of participants fell to 26 percent; almost a 50 percent dropout rate. Why? According to Ewing and Seefeldt, the most important reasons children stop playing are as follows:

- I lost interest.
- I was not having fun.
- It took too much time.
- Coach was a poor teacher.
- Too much pressure.
- Wanted more sport activity.
- I was tired of it.
- Needed more study time.
- Coach played favorites.
- Sport was boring.
- Overemphasis on winning.

become successful in sports and become champions are impatient and want it now! They do not want to wait four to six years; they want it as quickly as possible. Competition organizers and boards of education can become positive elements in children's athletics, if they organize competitions according to children's potential by imposing age limits based on the proper age for children to participate in high-level competitions.

Competing Too Often

Coaches and instructors often try to duplicate the number of games professional athletes play. Take, for instance, ice hockey in Canada or soccer in the United States. In ice hockey, children of 8 to 10 years old play anywhere from 60 to 80 games per season. The logic goes like this: professional players play 80 games per season, so if you want to become a professional player you have to do what professional athletes do!

By contrast, when the Soviet system of training was in full swing (1950s-1980s), team sports had a four-to-one training session to game ratio. This means children had four training sessions to work on skills and developing motor abilities to every game. Here in North America, in some team sports children are lucky if they get a one-to-one ratio. In ice hockey, the ratio is outrageous at three games to one practice! When do these children have the time to work on their skills and fitness?

Often, in team sports, such as ice hockey, baseball, soccer, or basketball, children attend weekend tournaments. In these circumstances the ratio may be even worse than one-to-one. So, is there any wonder that the improvement rate is slow, and children are emotionally taxed far beyond their tolerance level?

In individual sports, such as track and field, gymnastics, and skiing, although not necessarily swimming, the situation is far better. The ratio in these sports is often 8- or 10-to-1 or more.

We must be aware that early success offers no promise of the same later on and does not guarantee future stardom. Success during childhood means more competition, which leads to psychological stress and failure in skill proficiency. The higher the number of games the children play, the lower the number of practices, which means skill proficiency decreases and weaker performances. It is essential that children practice more and compete less.

Emphasizing Winning

If our prime interest is to develop talented athletes, then it is essential for us to emphasize *skill development* and de-emphasize *winning* in sports programs for children.

Emphasis on winning creates situations that are too stressful for children to adequately develop skill. Instead, they are often reinforcing and further developing skills that are technically incorrect.

The best way for children to develop skills is to practice them in a fun, nonstressful, nonthreatening environment. Such an environment seldom exists within competitive sports programs. In many cases, children are competing too frequently and have little time available to practice the necessary skills that will help them become better athletes.

In some leagues, such as hockey, in which young children have to compete in as many as 80 games a season, they devote little time to skill development. During games children are *applying*, not *developing*, their skills. If children have not

© Victah Sailer

properly developed their skills before application, they will be reinforcing poor techniques and unquestionably developing bad habits.

Once children develop bad technical habits they are difficult to correct. Children must have the opportunity to develop skills properly before they apply them in a competitive environment. Otherwise, they will likely develop skills that may be suitable for success at their particular stage of development, but not suitable for higher levels of competition.

For example, let's assume a coach wants to develop a top-notch 10-year-old amateur wrestler. The coach may encourage the child to learn some fancy throws, which will provide the young wrestler with terrific opportunities for success as a 10-year-old. At 14 years old, however, the child will likely have a poor throwing technique, because at the earlier age he or she did not have sufficient strength and power to learn the technique properly. Instead of developing a strong fundamental technical base, the young wrestler spent too much time practicing throws. As a result, the young wrestler may become discouraged when, at 14 years old, other children are much better at performing the fundamental techniques necessary for wrestling success, such as basic leg attacks.

Discriminating Against Late Maturing Children

Coaches who want to win usually play their best players. Often, the best players are those who have matured early, because they are bigger, stronger, faster, and have more endurance. In such cases, early maturing children occupy starting positions on the sport teams, while late maturing children sit on the bench.

Early maturing children are undoubtedly better athletes during childhood. However, much research indicates that late maturing children may have greater potential to reach international standards in a specific sport during adulthood. In fact, in the 1980s, in their quest to dominate the athletic world, the former communist countries of Eastern Europe switched their selection of talented children from early maturing children to late maturing children. Experience had shown that their practice of selecting early maturing children had only sometimes met their expectations. The late maturing children, however, displayed more consistency and, in most cases, achieved higher performance levels.

The adolescent growth spurt of late maturing children starts at a later stage of development and lasts longer than that of early maturing children. As a result, when late maturing children reach adulthood, their athletic development is usually better than early maturing children. Unfortunately, in many sports programs for children, late maturing children do not get equal opportunities to participate, because of the overemphasis on winning. These children are discriminated against in many situations.

Risking Injury

Although the stress of intensive training that is demanding physically and taxing psychologically may result in burnout, it also often results in injuries. In many instances, children are not exposed to training programs that have a long-term perspective. On the contrary, parents and coaches want quick results. To achieve this, the coach does not pay much attention to strengthening the anatomy of the children. When the coach ignores the condition of ligaments, tendons, cartilage, and muscle tissue, the injury-prevention portion of a program is often missing. This shortcoming, added to high-intensity training, can only result in injuries.

Nutrition for Training and Competition

Young athletes need good nutrition to maintain health, and optimize athletic performance. In addition, their nutrition must provide for physical growth and development. Coaches and parents need to stay on top of their young athletes' diets and ensure they are meeting their nutrition and fluid needs.

The Food Guide Pyramid

What is proper nutrition? Nutrition guidelines published by the U.S. Department of Agriculture are illustrated in the Food Guide Pyramid, shown on page 180. The pyramid divides food into six classifications and recommends the number of required servings for the average person older than three years. Contrary to popular belief, recommendations for athletes do not vary greatly from the average; the greatest difference for athletes is in portion size or total number of calories consumed per day. As athletes are more active than their sedentary counterparts, they naturally require more energy for their daily activities.

The Food Guide Pyramid suggests that children should consume a minimum of half of their daily calories from carbohydrates. When the body digests carbohydrates, energy in the form of glucose is produced, which is necessary for all forms of physical activity. As you can see, the Food Guide Pyramid recommends that 6 to 11 servings of carbohydrate foods be consumed each day. Examples of carbohydrate foods are breads, cereals, rice, and pasta. It is recommended that 3 to 5 servings of vegetables be consumed each day, along with 2 to 4 servings of fruit.

In addition to carbohydrate foods, fruits, and vegetables, the body needs protein, found in such foods as milk, yogurt, cheese, meat, poultry, fish, beans, eggs, and nuts. The U.S. Department of Agriculture recommends that 2 to 3 servings of dairy be consumed daily, along with 2 to 3 servings of meat, poultry, fish, beans, eggs, and nuts. It's important to consume protein as it helps to repair and maintain body tissue. Protein also produces hemoglobin, which carries oxygen to cells.

Fats, oils, and sweets are not to be excluded from the diet. Fats help the body absorb vitamins and are important for the formation of cell membranes. Unsaturated and monounsaturated fats such as safflower, corn, peanut, and olive oils are much preferred over saturated fats such as beef fat and butter. It's recommended that 30 percent or less of daily calories come from fats, with only 10 percent consisting of saturated fats.

Dehydration

Dehydration in young athletes is very common, and is detrimental to health and athletic performance. Water plays an essential part in athletic performance as it regulates and athlete's body temperature, transports nutrients, oxygen, and waste to plasma, and is necessary for energy production. Unfortunately, thirst is not a good indicator of fluid needs, as dehydration has usually already occurred before the athlete feels thirsty, therefore athletes must be encouraged to drink frequently. Ensure athletes begin the training session or competition fully hydrated. They should drink about 10 to 14 ounces of fluid 1 to 2 hours before an athletic event and another 10 ounces 10 to 15 minutes prior to competition. Encourage athletes to drink an additional 3 to 4 ounces every 15 minutes during the event.

After an event, an athlete should drink 16 ounces of cold water for every pound of weight he or she has lost through sweat. Sport drinks may be consumed in place of water, and in fact may be preferred by young athletes. It is recommended that these rehydration fluids should contain 6 to 8 percent carbohydrates. Carbohydrates provide athletes with needed fuel and may aid athletes engaged in endurance events.

Athletes at Prepuberty

During prepubescence parents will notice a decrease in their child's growth rate, maturation of fine and gross motor skills, and a change in appetite. Children may change the amount of food they eat each meal, refuse to eat meats and vegetables, or want to eat the same foods day after day. Any of the aforementioned behaviors should be expected.

Changes in personality and outside influences may alter eating patterns and preferred foods, but children should consistently consume three balanced meals per day, with two or three small, healthy snacks between meals.

Athletes at Puberty

Along with the physical growth and maturation during puberty comes an elevated nutritional require-

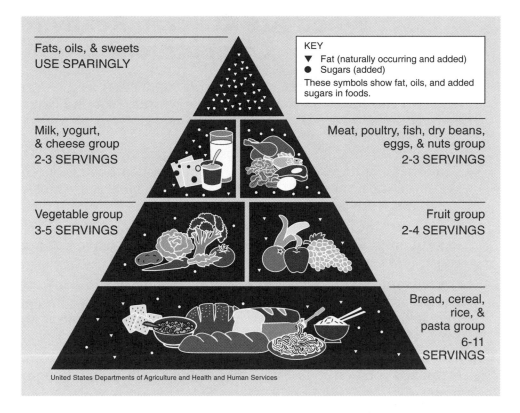

Fats, oils, & sweets
USE SPARINGLY

KEY
▼ Fat (naturally occurring and added)
● Sugars (added)
These symbols show fat, oils, and added sugars in foods.

Milk, yogurt,
& cheese group
2-3 SERVINGS

Meat, poultry, fish, dry beans,
eggs, & nuts group
2-3 SERVINGS

Vegetable group
3-5 SERVINGS

Fruit group
2-4 SERVINGS

Bread, cereal,
rice, &
pasta group
6-11
SERVINGS

United States Departments of Agriculture and Health and Human Services

ment. Both genders acquire 40 to 45 percent of their bone mass during puberty, so vitamin D and calcium (about 1,200 mg per day) are necessary to ensure proper bone growth. Milk is one of the most calcium rich foods in the diet. Common adolescent deficiencies, such as inadequate iron and calcium levels, are often due to insufficient intakes of vegetables and meats.

Adolescents active in sport require an estimated 600 to 1,500 more calories per day than nonactive teens, but excessive protein consumption or carbohydrate loading is not recommended during this stage. Extra calories will not aid in athletic performance or rapidly increase lean muscle mass; instead they will be stored as fat.

During puberty, 45 to 50 percent of daily calories should be derived from carbohydrates, which provide the fuel needed for exercise. Fats should total less than 30 percent of daily caloric intake. Protein, necessary for the growth and development of the adolescent body and found in red meat, chicken, fish, beans, and eggs, should make up about 15 percent of the diet. Most sources of protein are also sources of iron, necessary for the increased blood volume that occurs during puberty. Adolescent boys should consume about 12 mg of iron per day and girls about 15 mg daily. Female athletes may consume up to 30 mg of iron a day to maintain adequate iron levels. Iron supplies by animal sources are easily consumed by the body and is referred to as heme iron.

A puberty growth spurt in girls results in a greater increase in adipose tissue and a smaller increase in lean muscle. For boys, the growth spurt results in more lean muscle mass and less fat than for girls, but the growth pattern for boys is different. Boys often gain height before weight. Parents and coaches must not stress physically demanding sports before the body is ready. When weight is gained, through gains in muscle mass, it will be accompanied by strength. Skill formation, not strength, should be the focus of training until maturation is complete.

Athletes at Postpuberty

During this phase, carbohydrate-loading techniques, excessive protein intakes, and other methods of using nutrition to obtain a competitive advantage are introduced. Each sport and athlete will require different nutritional advice. Use the pyramid as a guideline to ensure that foods from all food groups are consumed with the basic nutritional requirements being met.

173

When Are Children Ready for Competition?

In most cases, it is not the children who ask to enter competitions, but the parents and coaches. I ask those who make decisions for children to participate in competitions to keep these guidelines in mind.

- Enter children in competitions only when they are ready. This includes motivational readiness (they want to compete), demonstration of an appropriate skill level, and an appropriate level of physiological capacity (motor abilities needed to be competitive).

- Ensure the primary goals are to have fun; learn skills; and reach certain skill, tactical, or physical objectives, such as, "If you have five good passes during the game, I'll be happy."

- Organize skills competitions for individual sports. For instance, "Whoever has the nicest skill will win," whether it be running, swimming, rowing, or skiing. Skill emphasis will be beneficial later, and it takes away the physiological stress of competitions and the need to train hard.

- Discourage children younger than seven or eight years from participating in organized competitions. They can test their skills in a noncompetitive environment.

- Only at 12 to 13 years do children understand the role of competition and what it takes, from the point of view of skills and abilities, to experience success or failure. Therefore, participation in organized competition should begin in the late elementary school years of 11 or 12 years and later.

Table 8.1 illustrates some guidelines for the age of entering competitions and offers suggestions about the number of competitions per year. Please note the difference between team and individual sports. For individual sports, the num-

Table 8.1	Suggested Types and Number of Competitions for Children	
Age	Types of competitions	Number of organized competitions per year
4-7	No formal competition, just for fun.	—
8-11	Informal competitions, stress skill form rather than winning. Participate in other sports, just for fun.	Team sports: 5-10
12-13	Participate in organized competitions in which the goal is to achieve certain physical, technical, or tactical goals, rather than winning.	Team sports: 10-15 Individual sports: 5-8
14-16	Participate in competitions without pushing to reach the best performance possible.	Team sports: 15-20 Individual sports: 8-10
17-19	Participate in junior competitions to qualify for state and national championships. Get ready to reach peak performance at the senior competitions.	Team sports: 20-35 Individual sports: Short duration: 20-30 Long duration: 6-8

ber refers to the number of starts (heats) and not the number of competitions (i.e., in the 100-meter sprint, you may have three heats per competition: heats, semifinals, and finals).

Preventing Stress and Burnout

Stress is usually perceived as an unpleasant emotional reaction to threatening situations or failure to meet performance expectations. Competitions expose young athletes to stress, especially for individual sports, in which teammates cannot share stress. Regardless of the level of competition, excessive stress has negative consequences, such as insomnia, loss of appetite, and sickness before competitions.

The pressure of winning, which comes from both the parents and the coaches, aggravates the degree of stress children experience. The stress level children experience is higher if the love and approval of parents is contingent on performing well. This pressure, coming from parents, coaches, and peers, is in most cases too much to cope with, especially for young children. Although training specialists and researchers often refer to the negative effects of competition stress, they do not emphasize understanding the strain and pain children experience in the training sessions preceding important competitions. Often, these workouts produce negative effects similar to those of competitions. Moderate levels of stress, however, can provide a setting that enhances children's motivation and performance.

Competitive-related stress is manifested before, during, and after competition.

• Precompetitive stress manifests itself in fears about not doing well, fear that your contribution to the team's performance will not meet the expectations of teammates, sleeping disorders, restlessness, frequent urination, and diarrhea.

• During competition stress manifests itself in fear of making mistakes, failure to take chances, poor performance due to high anxiety, sensitivity to coaches or teammates' criticism, lack of energy, paleness, and trembling.

• Postcompetitive stress (manifested after losing a game or after a poor performance) is demonstrated by lethargy, depression, moodiness, irritability, isolating self from family and peers, lack of appetite, sleeping disorders, and lack of willingness to train or to show up for the first workout.

Burnout is the result of chronic stress induced in training and competitions and may include lack of energy, exhaustion, sleeplessness, irritability, physical ailments, headaches, anger, loss of confidence, depression, and a decrease in performance achievement. Some victims of burnout drop out from further participation in sports.

You can prevent both stress and burnout to a high degree if you use the following techniques (Rotella, Hanson, and Coop, 1991):

• Have a good time in training and competitions. Enjoy being with your friends, and improving your skills. Set goals for yourself not directly related to the outcome of competition.
• Separate overall self-esteem from performance (especially for specific tasks). Failure to win the game does not depend strictly on you. Set goals for

175

yourself that you can achieve. As long as you have achieved your own goals, be satisfied.

- Develop interests other than the chosen sport. Your life and satisfaction with life must not be strictly dependent on the performance you achieve in your sport. Have hobbies: listen to music, paint, socialize, and find other reasons to be happy.
- Play a sport recreationally. Just for the fun of it!
- Take time to relax, enjoy family and friends.
- Remember that the sport is just a game.
- Learn to laugh at yourself, accept and learn from your errors and failures, and enjoy your successes. Sports are just one of many environments in which you are involved. An eventual loss of a game can easily be offset by the satisfaction you have in other areas.

Suggestions for coaches to help athletes avoid burnout include the following:

- Watch for the signs of staleness (i.e., lack of enthusiasm, irritability, decrease in performance).
- Provide variety and fun in training.
- Help the athletes have balance in their lives.
- Encourage athletes to have nonsport interests.
- Keep sports in perspective (for the athletes and yourself).
- More importantly, emphasize the goal of doing certain skills well, rather than performance.

You can also avoid stress and burnout by alternating training with other activities. You may use tables 8.2 and 8.3 as guidelines for planning children's weekly activities.

Monitoring Training

Children's participation in competitions requires ongoing assessment, including medical supervision by a physician and monitoring by parents and coaches. To properly assess athletes' improvements and reactions to training, every coach and parent should employ, as scientifically as possible, monitoring techniques. Some coaches and clubs have access (and financial means) to laboratories that can administer physiological, psychological, and biomechanical testing to evalu-

Table 8.2	**Weekly Schedule With Three Training Sessions**					
Monday	**Tuesday**	**Wednesday**	**Thursday**	**Friday**	**Saturday**	**Sunday**
Training	Free for socializing with friends	Training	Free for play and games	Training	Recreational sports or hobbies	Off

Table 8.3	Weekly Schedule With Four Training Sessions					
Monday	**Tuesday**	**Wednesday**	**Thursday**	**Friday**	**Saturday**	**Sunday**
Training	Training	Free for socializing with friends	Training	Training	Recreational sports or hobbies	Off

ate athletes' improvements, performance, efficiency, technical effectiveness, and mental power. Others do not have such opportunities. Irrespective of testing opportunities, the proposed simple and practical monitoring charts are useful for each athlete, because you perform organized testing just a few times a year. Between these times, you can monitor training randomly or not at all. This is why I am suggesting simple methods of assessing athletes' improvements. The tests in this section are simple for parents and instructors to organize. By keeping records of each test, you will be able to monitor the improvements of your child or athlete.

Throughout a training program, a coach must have some feedback about the load used in training. Such feedback can be physiological and psychological, and you can record it daily on the following charts. The first chart, which shows the heart rate, allows the parent and coach to monitor training physiologically, whereas the other reflects the psychological reactions.

There are two sets of daily charts. The first is an example, and the blank one you can photocopy and use for your child or athlete's needs. As you can see in the top of the chart, there is a space to write the name of the athlete and the month of the year. Each chart is designed for 31 days, and you can use it for the maximum number of days in a month. Each athlete should fill in the chart daily. He or she can keep it at home, in the bedroom, and preferably in a log book, so the parents can see the records, and the athlete can take it to training sessions to show the instructor.

It is essential that the coach look at the charts of each athlete before a training session, to change the training program according to the athlete's psychological state and fatigue level. For instance, if the heart rate chart indicates a high level of fatigue, or the length of sleep chart shows just four hours of restless sleep, then the daily program must be easy, with no high intensity, which normally increases the fatigue.

Heart Rate Chart

Heart rate is useful for monitoring the athlete's reaction to the previous day's training program. Before using the heart rate chart on page 180, the athlete must know his or her *base heart rate (BHR),* which is the heart rate taken in the morning before stepping out of bed. To determine the heart rate, count the number of pulse beats for 10 seconds, then multiply this number by 6.

Take a blank chart and place a dot in the number 1 column, in the lower one-third of the chart, and record the value of the heart rate (i.e., 53 on the sample chart). From this number, complete the numbers to the top and bottom of the column.Continue to take the BHR daily, entering a dot in the appropriate line of the next column, and joining it to the previous dot to form a curve.

The BHR also reacts to the intensity of the previous day's training. When the BHR increases by six to eight beats per minute over the standard curve in one day, it could mean that the previous day's training program was not well tolerated or that the athlete did not observe a normal athletic lifestyle. For example, the athlete may be fatigued from illness, or he is too tired from staying up late and not getting enough sleep. The coach should find out the reason from the athlete, and, in whatever case, change the planned training program so it does not add to an already high level of fatigue. When the curve decreases to its standard levels, the normal program can resume.

The BHR illustrates the athlete's physiological state and reaction to training. Under normal conditions, the curve does not have many deflections. The dynamics of the curve could change, however, according to the training phase and the state of the athlete's adaptation to the training program. As an athlete adapts to training, the BHR curve drops progressively, and the better the adaptation the lower the curve. Certainly, the curve depends on the chosen sport. Usually athletes from endurance-dominant sports have lower BHR levels.

Psychological Traits and Appetite Chart

The athlete must also complete each element of this chart daily (see page 182). These charts have a high correlation to the heart chart. When an athlete experiences a high degree of fatigue, then sleeping patterns are disturbed and appetite decreases, which correlates with tiredness sensation, and training and competitive willingness. All these decrease as the level of fatigue or overtraining increase.

The sample chart on page 181 represents a real-life situation of an athlete training to compete in the Olympic Games. By adequately changing the training program and improving the diet, which included supplements, the athlete recuperated and competed in the games as expected (fourth place).

These simple and practical charts for monitoring training are useful for the serious athlete. You can prevent many undesirable situations by filling them in every day and having the coach examine them before every training session. Spending a minute a day may help an athlete avoid overtraining.

Sample Heart Rate Chart

Heart rate	1	2	3	4	5	6	7	8	9	10	11	12	13	14	15	16	17	18	19	20	21	22	23	24	25	26	27	28	29	30	31
72																															
71																															
70																															
69																															
68																															
67																															
66																															
65																															
64																															
63																															
62																															
61																															
60																															
59																															
58																															
57																															
56																															
55																															
54																															
53																															
52																															
51																															
50																															
49																															
48																															
47																															
46																															
45																															
44																															
43																															

Heart Rate Chart

Heart rate	1	2	3	4	5	6	7	8	9	10	11	12	13	14	15	16	17	18	19	20	21	22	23	24	25	26	27	28	29	30	31
72																															
71																															
70																															
69																															
68																															
67																															
66																															
65																															
64																															
63																															
62																															
61																															
60																															
59																															
58																															
57																															
56																															
55																															
54																															
53																															
52																															
51																															
50																															
49																															
48																															
47																															
46																															
45																															
44																															
43																															

Sample Psychological Traits and Appetite Chart

Name _____   Month _____

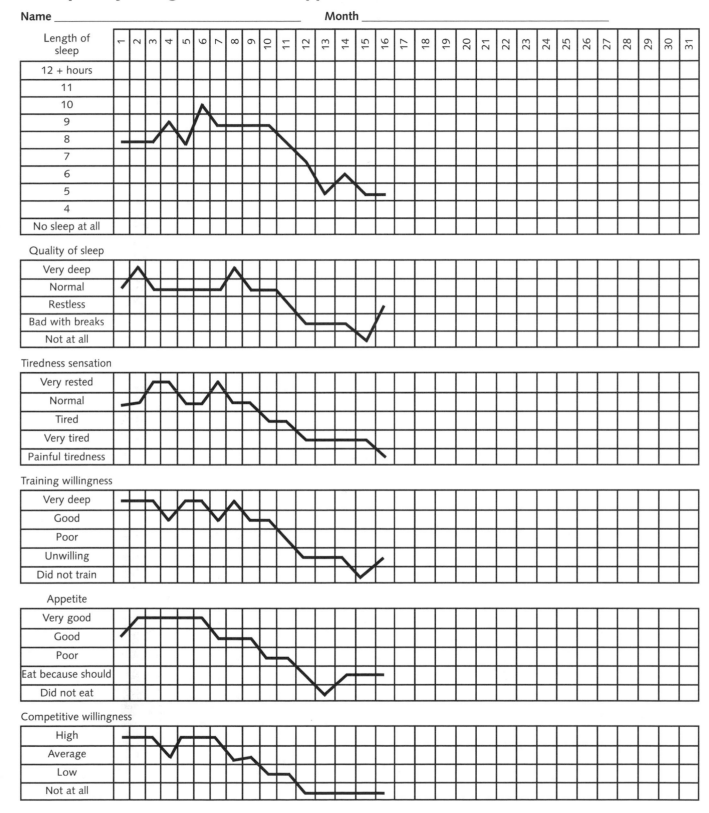

Psychological Traits and Appetite Chart

Name _____   Month _____

Length of sleep	1	2	3	4	5	6	7	8	9	10	11	12	13	14	15	16	17	18	19	20	21	22	23	24	25	26	27	28	29	30	31
12 + hours																															
11																															
10																															
9																															
8																															
7																															
6																															
5																															
4																															
No sleep at all																															

Quality of sleep

Very deep																															
Normal																															
Restless																															
Bad with breaks																															
Not at all																															

Tiredness sensation

Very rested																															
Normal																															
Tired																															
Very tired																															
Painful tiredness																															

Training willingness

Very deep																															
Good																															
Poor																															
Unwilling																															
Did not train																															

Appetite

Very good																															
Good																															
Poor																															
Eat because should																															
Did not eat																															

Competitive willingness

High																															
Average																															
Low																															
Not at all																															

chapter 9

Long-Term Training Plans

Compiling a long-term training model is necessary for anyone involved in children's training. Such a model gives a basic guideline to follow. Although it may undergo changes or additions, the basic plan will be there, which will prevent rushing a children's program aimlessly like a ship with no rudder.

To take a child from prepuberty to late postpuberty with a logical progression, you will need this rudder, this long-term model, whether the plan is simple or complex.

In this chapter you will find long-term training models for 10 sports. You can examine the one that interests you, and either apply it as suggested or make changes and additions to suit your athlete's needs or the environment in which you work. If the sport you are interested in is not present, then create your own plan using another similar plan for a model.

The first plan is for a track sprinter, and I will explain this model so you can understand the process of compiling a training model.

Ages from six to athletic maturation are entered across the top of the chart. Training phases, which are already familiar to you, skill acquisition, and the way you must organize the motor ability training over the years are listed down the left side of the chart. Competition levels are listed at the bottom of the chart, along with the ages for entering athletes in each level.

The chart is divided by vertical lines that separate one type of activity from another. I either mention the type of training by a specific term or block it out. The latter case indicates the duration of that activity, for instance, from the age of 10 to 17.

The row showing skill acquisition refers to the progression of learning technical skills. In our example, the ultimate scope is to reach perfection. However, this will be impossible without first learning basic skills from age 6 to 12 years, followed by a phase from age 12 to 16 years, in which the goal is to repeat parts of skills or full skills for automation. For our purpose, automation means to learn a skill so well that a young athlete can perform it automatically at a consistently high level.

Skill formation is not a quick fix—it takes time and is acquired in several phases. In this early phase, a young athlete is exposed to the basic or fundamental skills of the chosen sport. During this phase a skill is often performed with some rigidity. The child often appears awkward and lacking decent coordination, because he is involuntarily involving some muscles that are not necessary for the particular action. Depending on the child's background and natural coordination, this phase could be a relatively short one or it could last up to two years.

Following the first few years of technical teaching the athletes begin to feel familiar with the skills and start to perform them with ease. This is the time of skill automation: a skill—no matter how difficult—starts to be performed automatically in a very natural way. Now only the prime movers (the actual muscles used in the performance of the skill) are contracted, therefore the action is performed smoothly, with ease and a natural flow.

From this skill automation stage and on, the instructor starts to work on skill perfection. Skill perfection, often called the highlight of athletic mastery, is achieved when skills of high difficulty are performed fast, with great finesse, and with maximum efficiency.

The acquisition of tactical skills, especially for team sports, also takes time because they are performed in a certain progression. As soon as an athlete is capable of performing the basic technical skills, she is progressively exposed to simple individual tactics. These skills are often position-related, meaning that the child must learn and perform the tactics specific to a given position in that particular sport.

The next phase begins as soon as a child is comfortable with the tactical skills required for a given position. Here the coach teaches the athletes how to apply their individual tactics to the team setting. Since team tactics change depending on the strategies applied by the opposition, the team's tactics must be applied with flexibility. Now the young athletes are required to adjust their own skills according to the specifics of the game and the game environment, such as weather, wind, temperature, and so on.

I would also like to advise all coaches to expose their players to different positions in the early years of training. The better a player can perform in other positions, the easier it will be for him to switch positions at a later date if he so desires. In the early years no one knows whether a player's best position is on the offense or the defense. This is why a young athlete should play several positions. Only in the late teens, during the years of specialization, should players be placed in a position where they have the highest game effectiveness.

A large part of the chart refers to training the required physical abilities. This starts with coordination, performing simple skills at first, progressing to more complex skills through the middle teens, and ultimately performing the skills as perfectly as possible.

Flexibility comes next, with children spending the early years of athletic involvement between 6 and 14 developing the best possible flexibility for all joints of the body, emphasizing sport-specific flexibility from 14 to 18 but still maintaining all-around flexibility. When children develop flexibility in this way, after the age of 18 they can dedicate time to maintaining what they have achieved. It is always easier to maintain a given level than to develop it.

The focus on developing agility is during puberty and postpuberty, then on maintaining it thereafter. As suggested earlier, children can develop agility by performing specific exercises and drills, and they can influence it directly by repeating sport-specific exercises. Another positive influence on agility is repeating many drills and exercises to develop speed and power. ·

Speed training for sprinting consists of two elements, linear acceleration (straight speed) and starts. Linear acceleration is displayed immediately after the start, reaching maximum velocity around 40-60 m/yards. From 80 m/yards on, the ability to maintain high velocity depends on how well speed-endurance is trained (please refer to the discussion on speed training in chapter 5). A good start is a skill to be learned and it depends on one's reaction time. Good starts improve as a result of learning and practicing the skill. Strength training, on the other hand, starts with informal repetitions of simple exercises as suggested for prepuberty, followed by periodizing it over the year. This starts with anatomical adaptation

(in this case, 10 to 18 years), muscular endurance, power, and finally maximum strength. This sequence of strength-training types follows an obvious progression from low to high loads, with the highest being for maximum strength from the age of 18 onward. By the time a young athlete experiences heavy loads (maximum strength), he or she will have eight years of background with lower loads. Such a progression ensures a good and long adaptation resulting in an injury-free athlete.

The endurance component of training also follows a long-term progression from general endurance to aerobic, and ultimately to anaerobic. Anaerobic is the most taxing training type for any athletes, and especially young ones.

Finally, everybody involved in training young athletes should realize that there is also a progression for competition. For a child to enjoy sports, it is not important that he or she compete often and in stressful competitions. Please remember that winning at the age of 10 does not guarantee that the same athlete will be winning at the age of maturation. Most often the opposite is true. Participation in competitions during the early years should have just one scope—enjoyment and fun! As the child grows older, becomes more skillful, and better trained, he or she may progressively participate in local, state, and national competitions. Certainly some athletes who follow the long-term program will excel in a given sport and compete in international or professional sports.

TRACK AND FIELD, SPRINTING

	AGE
	6 7 8 9 10 11 12 13 14 15 16 17 18 19 20 21 22 25 30 35

TRAINING PHASES	Initiation	Athl. form.	Spec.	High performance	

Skill acquisition	Technical	Basic skill		Auto.	Perfection	

	Coordination	Simple	Complex	Perfection	
	Flexibility	Overall	Specific	Maintain	
T	Agility		(shaded)	Maintain	
r	Speed — Linear		(shaded)		
a	Speed — Reaction time	Starts		Perfection	
i	Strength — Anatomical adaptation		(shaded)		
n	Strength — Muscular endurance		(shaded)		
i	Strength — Power		(shaded)		
n	Strength — Maximum strength		(shaded)		
g	Endurance — General		(shaded)		
	Endurance — Anaerobic		(shaded)		
C	Fun		(shaded)		
o	Local		(shaded)		
m	State/provincial		(shaded)		
p	National		(shaded)		
	International/ professional		(shaded)		

LEGEND: Shaded area shows the age to start or end the work on that ability.
Athl. form. = Athletic formation.
Spec. = Specialization in a given event(s).
Auto. = Skill automation.
Comp. = Competitions.

TRACK AND FIELD, THROWS AND JUMPS

		AGE			
		6 7 8 9 10 11 12 13 14	15 16 17	18 19 20 21 22	25 30 35
TRAINING PHASES		Initiation	Athl. form.	Spec.	High performance
Skill acquisition	Technical	Basic skills: run, jump, throw	Auto.	Perfection	
	Coordination	Simple	Complex	Perfection	
	Flexibility	Overall		Specific	Maintain
T	Agility		■	■	Maintain
r	Speed — Linear		■	■	
a	Speed — Reaction time		■	■	
i	Strength — Anatomical adaptation		■		
n	Strength — Power			■	
i	Strength — Maximum strength			■	
n	Endurance — General	■			
g	Endurance — Anaerobic		■		
C	Fun	■			
o	Local		■		
m	State/provincial		■		
p	National			■	
	International/ professional			■	

Note: Early years competitions are for relays and multievents.

LEGEND: Athl. form. = Athletic formation.
Spec. = Specialization in a given event(s).
Auto. = Skill automation.
Comp. = Competitions.

BASEBALL

			AGE 6–35
			6 7 8 9 10 11 12 13 14 15 16 17 18 19 20 21 22 25 30 35

TRAINING PHASES			Initiation · Athl. form · Spec. · High perf.
Skill acquisition	Technical		Fundamentals · Position specific · Position–and game–specific
Skill acquisition	Tactical		Simple game strategy · Game strategy · Position/game strategy
Training	Coordination		Simple · Complex · Perfection
Training	Flexibility		Overall · Specific · Maintain
Training	Agility		Maintain
Training	Speed	Linear	
Training	Speed	Turns/ changes in directions	
Training	Speed	Reaction time	
Training	Strength	Anatomical adaptation	
Training	Strength	Power	
Training	Strength	Maximum strength	
Training	Endurance	General	
Training	Endurance	Anaerobic	
Comp.	Fun		
Comp.	Local		
Comp.	State/provincial		
Comp.	National		
Comp.	International/ professional		

LEGEND: Athl. form. = Athletic formation.
Spec. = Specialization in a given event(s).
High perf. = High performance.
Comp. = Competitions

189

BASKETBALL

<table>
<tr><th colspan="3">BASKETBALL</th></tr>
</table>

		AGE
		6 7 8 9 10 11 12 13 14 15 16 17 18 19 20 21 22 25 30 35

TRAINING PHASES		Initiation	Athl. form	Spec.	High perf.

| Skill acquisition | Technical | Basic skills | | Auto. | Perfection |
| | Tactical | Simple indiv. tactics | | F. of T. ta. | Perfection |

	Coordination	Simple	Complex	Perfection
	Flexibility	Overall	Specific	Maintain

Training

- Agility
- Speed
  - Linear
  - Turns/changes in directions
  - Reaction time
- Strength
  - Anatomical adaptation
  - Muscular endurance
  - Power
  - Maximum strength
- Endurance
  - General
  - Aerobic
  - Anaerobic

Comp

- Fun
- Local
- State/provincial
- National
- International/professional

LEGEND: Athl. form. = Athletic formation.
Auto. = Skill automation.
F. of T. ta. = Foundation of team tactics.
Spec. = Specialization in a given event (s).
Comp. = Competitions.
High perf. = High performance.

FOOTBALL																									
		AGE																							
		6	7	8	9	10	11	12	13	14	15	16	17	18	19	20	21	22	25	30	35		
TRAINING PHASES		Initiation						Mini-football				H.S.		Spec.				High perf.					
Skill acquisition	Technical					Fundamentals						Auto.				Perfection game–specific							
	Tactical					Simple rules						Game tactics				Position–specific tactics							
Coordination					Simple						Complex				Perfection								
Flexibility					Overall								Specific			Maintenance							

GYMNASTICS (WOMEN)

	6	7	8	9	10	11	12	13	14	15	16	17	18	19	20
TRAINING PHASES	Initiation			Athl. form.			Spec.			High perf.					
Skill acquisition / Technical	Skill form.				Auto.		Perfection								
Coordination	Simple				Complex		Perfection								
Flexibility	OV.		Shou./hips		Maintenance										
Training — Agility				█	█	█	█	█	█	Maintain					
Training — Speed / Linear				█	█	█	█	█	█	█	█	█	█	█	█
Training — Strength / Anatomical adaptation							█	█	█	█	█	█	█	█	█
Training — Strength / Power					█	█	█	█	█	█	█	█	█	█	█
Training — Strength / Maximum strength (men)											█	█	█	█	█
Training — Endurance / Anaerobic				█	█	█	█	█	█	█	█	█	█	█	█
Comp — Fun			█	█	█	█	█	█	█	█	█	█	█	█	█
Comp — Local					█	█	█	█	█	█	█	█	█	█	█
Comp — State/provincal							█	█	█	█	█	█	█	█	█
Comp — National										█	█	█	█	█	█
Comp — International/professional												█	█	█	█

LEGEND:
Athl. form. = Athletic formation.
Spec. = Specialization.
Skill form. = Skill formation.
Auto. = Skill automation.
OV. = Overall
Shou. = Shoulders
Comp. = Competitions.
High perf. = High performance

ICE HOCKEY

			AGE																				
			6	7	8	9	10	11	12	13	14	15	16	17	18	19	20	21	22	25	30	35
TRAINING PHASES			Initiation									Athl. form.		Spec.		High perf.						
Skill acquisition	Technical		Fundamental									Auto.		Perfection game/position–specific								
	Tactical		Simple indiv. tactics								Game tactics				Game position specific tactics							
Training	Coordination		Simple								Complex				Perfection							
	Flexibility		Overall								Specific				Maintain							
	Agility																					
	Speed	Linear																				
		Turns/ changes in directions																				
		Reaction time																				
	Strength	Anatomical adaptation																				
		Muscular endurance																				
		Power																				
		Maximum strength																				
	Endurance	General																				
		Aerobic																				
		Anaerobic																				
Comp.	Fun																					
	Local																					
	State/provincial																					
	National																					
	International/ professional																					

LEGEND: Athl. form. = Athletic formation.
Spec. = Specialization
Auto. = Skill automation.
High perf. = High performance
Comp. = Competitions.

SOCCER																						

AGE

			6	7	8	9	10	11	12	13	14	15	16	17	18	19	20	21	22	25	30	35

| TRAINING PHASES | | | | | Mini-soccer | | | | Novice | | Junior | | | High performance | | | | | | | |

| Skill acquisition | Technical | | Fundamentals | | | | | | Auto. | | | Perfection game/position–specific | | | |
| | Tactical | | | Simple rules | | | | | Game tactics | | | Game/position–specific tactics | | | |

| | Coordination | | | Simple | | | | Complex | | | Perfection | | | |
| | Flexibility | | | Overall | | | | Specific | | | Maintain | | | |

Training

Agility		
Speed	Linear	
	Turns/changes in directions	
	Reaction time	
Strength	Anatomical adaptation	
	Muscular endurance	
	Power	
	Maximum strength	
Endurance	General	
	Aerobic	
	Anaerobic	

Comp

Fun	
Local	
State/provincial	
National	
International/professional	

LEGEND: Auto. = Skill automation.
Comp. = Competitions.

SWIMMING

		AGE																
		6	7	8	9	10	11	12	13	14	15	16	17	18	19	20	21	22
TRAINING PHASES		Initiation								Athl. form.	Spec.			High perf.				
Skill acquisition	Technical	Basic skill								Auto.	Perfection							
	Tactical							Start			Even splits							
T **r** **a** **i** **n** **i** **n** **g**	Coordination	Simple								Com.	Perfection							
	Flexibility	Overall								Spe.	Maintenance							
	Agility																	
	Speed — Linear																	
	Speed — Turns/changes in direction																	
	Speed — Reaction time						Starts			Perfection								
	Strength — Anatomical adaptation																	
	Strength — Muscular endurance																	
	Strength — Power																	
	Strength — Maximum strength																	
	Endurance — General																	
	Endurance — Aerobic																	
	Endurance — Anaerobic																	
C **o** **m** **p**	Fun																	
	Local																	
	State/provincial																	
	National																	
	International/professional																	

LEGEND: Athl. form. = Athletic formation.
Spec. = Specialization.
Auto. = Skill automation.
Com. = Complex coordination.
Spe. = Specific.
High perf. = High performance.
Comp. = Competitions.

TENNIS

		AGE																			
		6	7	8	9	10	11	12	13	14	15	16	17	18	19	20	21	22	25	30	35
TRAINING PHASES		Initiation								Athl. form.		Spec.		High performance							
Skill acquisition	Technical	Basic skills										Auto.		Perfection							
	Tactical	Simple										Game tactics		Perfection							
Training	Coordination	Simple										Complex		Perfection							
	Flexibility	Overall										Specific		Maintenance							
	Agility																				
	Speed — Linear																				
	Speed — Turns/changes in directions																				
	Speed — Reaction time																				
	Strength — Anatomical adaptation																				
	Strength — Muscular endurance																				
	Strength — Power																				
	Strength — Maximum strength																				
	Endurance — General																				
	Endurance — Aerobic																				
	Endurance — Anaerobic																				
Comp	Fun																				
	Local																				
	State/provincial																				
	National																				
	International/professional																				

LEGEND: Athl. form. = Athletic formation.
Spec. = Specialization.
Auto. = Skill automation.
Comp. = Competitions.

VOLLEYBALL

		AGE
		6 7 8 9 10 11 12 13 14 15 16 17 18 19 20 21 22 25 30 35

TRAINING PHASES		Initiation	Athl. form.	Spec.	High performance

| Skill acquisition | Technical | | Bas. sk. | Auto. | Perfection |
| | Tactical | | Sim. ta. | F. of T. tactics | Perfection |

| Coordination | | Simple | Complex | Perfection |
| Flexibility | | Overall | Specific | Maintenance |

Training

Agility		
Speed	Linear	
	Turns/changes in directions	
	Reaction time	
Strength	Anatomical adaptation	
	Muscular endurance	
	Power	
	Maximum strength	
Endurance	General	
	Aerobic	
	Anaerobic	

Comp

Fun	
Local	
State/provincial	
National	
International/professional	

LEGEND: Athl. form. = Athletic formation.
Spec. = Specialization.
Bas. sk. = Basic skills.
Auto. = Skill automation.
Sim. ta. = Simple tactics.
F. of T. tactics = Foundation of team tactics.
Comp. = Competitions.

Bibliography

American Academy of Pediatrics. 1982. Risks in long-distance running for children, a statement. *The Physician and Sportsmedicine* 10: 82-83.

American Academy of Pediatrics. 1983. Weight training and weightlifting: Information for the pediatrician. *The Physician and Sportsmedicine* 11 (3): 157-161.

Anderson, A.B., K. Froberg, and O. Lammert. 1987. Should we revise our ideas of the effectiveness of youth training? *New Studies in Athletics* 1: 65-72.

Anshel, M.H., P. Freedman, J. Hamill, K. Haywood, M. Horvat, and S.A. Plowman. 1991. *Dictionary of the sport and exercise sciences.* Champaign, IL: Human Kinetics.

Armstrong, N., and B. Davies. 1984. The metabolic and physiological responses of children to exercise and training. *Physical Education* 7: 90-105.

Bailey, D.A. 1973. Exercise, fitness and physical education for the growing child. *Canadian Journal of Public Health* 64 (Sept./Oct.): 421-430.

Bailey, D.A., R.M. Malina, and R.L. Mirwald. 1985. The child, physical activity and growth. Pp. 147-170 in *Human growth*, Vol. 2, 2d ed., edited by F. Falkner and J.M. Tanner. New York: Plenum.

Baratta, R., M. Solomonow, B.H. Zhou, D. Letson, R. Chuinard, and R. Ambrosia. 1988. Muscular coactivation. The role of the antagonist musculature in maintaining knee stability. *American Journal of Sports Medicine* 16: 113-122.

Bar-Or, O. 1983. *Pediatric sports medicine for the practitioner.* New York: Springer-Verlag.

Bar-Or, O., and B. Goldberg. 1989. Trainability of the prepubescent child. *The Physician and Sportsmedicine* 17 (5)

Bompa, T. 1993a. *Periodization of strength: The new wave in strength training.* Toronto: Veritas.

Bompa, T. 1993b. *Power training for sport: Plyometrics for maximum power development.* Oakville, New York, London: Mosaic Press.

Bompa, T. 1994. *Theory and methodology of training.* Dubuque, IA: Kendall/Hunt.

Bompa, T. 1999. *Periodization: Theory and methodology of training,* 4th ed. Champaign, Illinois: Human Kinetics.

Bompa, T. 1999. *Periodization Training for Sports.* Champaign, IL: Human Kinetics.

Borms, J., and M. Hebbelinck. 1984. Review of studies on Olympic athletes. Pp. 7-27 in *Physical structure of Olympic athletes, Part II, Kinanthropometry of Olympic athletes. Medicine and sport science,* XVIII, edited by J.E.L. Carter. Basel: Karger.

Bowerman, R.W., and E.L. Fox. 1992. *Sports physiology.* Dubuque, IA: Brown.

Carlson, R. 1988. The socialization of elite tennis players in Sweden: An analysis of the players' backgrounds and development. *Sociology of Sport Journal* 5: 241-256.

Coakley, J. 1986. When should children begin competing? A sociological perspective. In *Sports for children and youths,* edited by M.R. Weiss and D. Gould. Champaign, IL: Human Kinetics.

Committee for the Development of Sport of the Council of Europe. 1982. *Conclusion of an International Seminar on Sport for Children*. Norway. Document CDDS (82).

Cureton, T.K., and M. Jette. 1976. Anthropometric and selected motor fitness measurement of men engaged in a long term program of physical activity. *Research Quarterly* 47: 666-667.

Docherty, D., and R.D. Bell. 1985. The relationship between flexibility and linearity measures in boys and girls 6-15 years of age. *Journal of Human Movement Studies* 11: 279-288.

Duda, M. 1986. Prepubescent strength training gains support. *The Physician and Sportsmedicine* 14 (2): 157-161.

Duquet, W., M. Hebbelinck, and J. Vajda. 1978. Biometrische studie van lichaamsbouwkenmerken vn Belgische langeafstandslopers (Biometrical study of body type characteristics of Belgian long distance runners). *Sport* (Extra Nummer: Sportwetenschappelijke bijdragen Brussel. BLOSO): 41-48.

Ewing, M.E., and V. Seefeldt. 1990. *American young and sports participation*. Youth Sports Institute of Michigan State University (sponsored by the Athletic Footwear Association, Palm Beach, FL).

Fleck, S.J., and J.E. Falkel. 1986. Value of resistance training for the reduction of sports injuries. *Sports Medicine* 3: 61-68.

Forbes, J.K. 1950. *Characteristics of flexibility in boys*. Doctoral diss., University of Oregon.

Forsyth, G. 1974. Burnout: Psychological or physiological? *Swimming Technique* 11 (1): 2-4, 20.

Fox, E.L., R.W. Bowers, and M.L. Foss. 1989. *The physiological basis of physical education and athletics*. Dubuque, IA: Brown.

Harre, D. 1982. *Trainingslehre*. Berlin: Sportverlag.

Harris, M.L. 1969. A factor analytic study of flexibility. *Research Quarterly* 40 (1): 62-70.

Hebbelinck, M. 1989. Development and motor performance. *Roma, Scuola dello Sport* VIII: 16.

Henschen, K.P. 1986. Athletic staleness and burnout: Diagnosis, prevention, and treatment. In *Applied sport psychology: Personal growth to peak performance*, edited by J. Williams. Palo Alto, CA: Mayfield.

Hughson, R. 1986. Children in competitive sports: A multi-disciplinary approach. *Canadian Journal of Applied Sport Science* 11 (4): 162-172.

Kabat, H. 1958. Proprioceptive facilitation in the therapeutic exercises. In *Therapeutic exercises*, edited by M.S. Licht. Baltimore: Waverly Press.

Kemper, H.C.G., and R. Verschuur. 1985. Motor performance fitness tests. In *Growth, health and fitness for teenagers. Longitudinal research in international perspective. Medicine and sport science, XX*, edited by H.C.G. Kemper. Basel: Karger.

Klafs, C.E., and D.D. Arnheim. 1977. *Modern principles of athletic training*. 4th ed. St. Louis: Mosby.

Kraemer, W.L., and S.J. Fleck. 1993. *Strength training for young athletes*. Champaign, IL: Human Kinetics.

Laubach, L.L., and J.T. McConville. 1966. Relationships between flexibility anthropometry, and the somatotype of college men. *Research Quarterly* 37 (2): 241-251.

Malina, R.M. 1984. Physical growth and maturation. In *Motor development during childhood and adolescence,* edited by J.R. Thomas. Minneapolis: Burgess.

Malina, R.M. 1986. Readiness for competitive youth sport. In *Sport for children and youths*, edited by M.R. Weiss and D. Gould. Champaign, IL: Human Kinetics.

Malina, R.M., and C. Bouchard. 1991. *Growth, maturation, and physical activity.* Windsor, ON: Human Kinetics.

Martens, R. 1978. *Joy and sadness in children's sports.* Champaign, IL: Human Kinetics.

Martens, R. 1981. Young sport in the USA. In *Children in sport,* 3d ed., edited by F.L. Smoll, R.A. Magill, and M.J. Ash. Champaign, IL: Human Kinetics.

Mason, T.A. 1970. Is weight lifting deleterious to the spines of young people? *British Journal of Sports Medicine* 5: 54-56.

Matsuda, J.J., R.F. Zernicke, A.C. Vailns, V.A. Pedrinin, A. Pedrini-Mille, and J.A. Maynard. 1986. Structural and mechanical adaptation of immature bone to strenuous exercise. *Journal of Applied Physiology* 60 (6): 2028-2034.

Matsui, H. 1983. Discovery of hereditary ability for junior athletes. *Asian Studies of Physical Education* 6 (1): 50-56.

McGovern, M.B. 1984. Effects of circuit weight training on the physical fitness of prepubescent children. *Dissertation Abstracts International* 45 (2): 452A-453A.

McGuire, R.T., and D.L. Cook. 1983. The influence of others and the decision to participate in youth sports. *Journal of Sport Behavior* 6: 9-16.

Micheli, L.J. 1988. Strength training in the young athlete. Pp. 99-105 in *Competitive sports for children and youth,* edited by E.W. Brown and C.E. Brants. Champaign, IL: Human Kinetics.

Nagorni, M.F. 1978. Facts and fiction regarding junior's training. *Fizkulturai Sport* 6

National Strength and Conditioning Association. Position paper on prepubescent children. Phd. diss., *Dissertation Abstracts International.* 7 (4):

Passer, M.W. 1988. Determinants and consequences of children's competitive stress. In *Children in sport,* 3d ed., edited by F.L. Smoll, R.A. Magill, and M.J. Ash. Champaign, IL: Human Kinetics.

Pechtl, V. 1982. The basic and methods of flexibility training. In *Trainingslehre,* edited by E. Harre. Berlin: Sportverlag.

Purdy, D.A., S. Haufler, and D.S. Eitzen. 1981. Stress among child athletes: Perceptions by parents, coaches, and athletes. *Journal of Sport Behavior* 4 (1): .

Ramsay, J.A., C.J.R. Blinikie, K. Smith, S. Garner, J.D. MacDougal, and D.G. Sale. 1990. Strength training effects in prepubescent boys. *Medicine and Science in Sports and Exercise* 22: 605-614.

Reiff, G.G., W.R. Dixon, D. Jacoby, X.G. Ye, C.G. Spain, and P.A. Hunsiker. 1985. President's Council on Physical Fitness and Sports. *National School Population Fitness Survey.* Ann Arbor, MI: University of Michigan.

Rians, C.B., A. Weltman, B.R. Cahill, C.A. Janney, S.R. Tippet, and F.I. Katch. 1987. Strength training for prepubescent males: Is it safe? *American Journal of Sports Medicine* 15: 483-489.

Roberts, D., A. Norton, A. Sinclair, and P. Lavkins. 1987. Children and long distance running. *New Studies in Athletics* 1: 7-8.

Roberts, G.C. 1986. The perception of stress: A potential source and its development. In *Sport for children and youths,* edited by M.R. Weiss and D. Gould. Champaign, IL: Human Kinetics.

Roberts, S.O., and D. Pillarella. 1996. *Developing strength in children: A comprehensive guide*. Reston, VA: American Alliance for Health, Physical Education, Recreation, and Dance (AAHPERD).

Ross, J.G., O. Dotson, G.G. Gilbert, and S.J. Katz. 1985. The national children and youth fitness study: New standards for fitness measurement. *Journal of Physical Education, Recreation and Dance* 56: 20-24.

Rotella, R.J., T. Hanson, and R.H. Coop. 1991. Burnout in youth and sports. *Elementary School Journal* 91(5).

Rovere, G.D. 1988. Low back pain in athletes. *The Physician and Sportsmedicine* 15: 105-117.

Rowland, T.W. 1989. Oxygen uptake and endurance fitness in children: A development perspective. *Pediatric Exercise Science* 1: 313-328.

Sailors, M., and K. Berg. 1987. Comparison of responses to weight training in pubescent boys and men. *Journal of Sports Medicine* 27: 30-37.

Sale, D.G. 1986. Neural adaptation in strength and power training. Pp. 281-305 in *Human muscle power,* edited by N.L. Jones, N. McCartney, and A.J. McComs. Champaign, IL: Human Kinetics.

Sapega, A.A., T.C. Quendenfeld, R.A. Moyer, and R.A. Butler. 1981. Biophysical factors in range of motion exercise. *The Physician and Sportsmedicine* 9: 57-65.

Schonberger, K. 1987. Young people and athletics in the GDR. *New Studies in Athletics* 1: 9-14.

Sharma, K.D., and P. Hirtz. 1991. The relationship between coordination quality and biological age. *Medicine and Sport* 31 (June): 3-4.

Shephard, R.J. 1982. *Physical activity and growth*. Chicago: Yearbook Medical.

Smith, T.K. 1984. Preadolescent strength training. Some considerations. *Journal of Physical Education, Recreation and Dance* 55: 43-44, 80.

Torbert, M., and L.B. Schnieder. 1986. Positive multicultural interaction: Using low organized games. *Journal of Physical Education, Recreation and Dance* (September): 40-44.

Weiskopf, D. 1974. Stretch to win. *Athletic Journal* (December): 32-34.

Yessis, K. 1988. *Secrets of Soviet sports fitness and training*. New York: Arbor House.

Index

A

acceleration training 73
adolescence and coordination development 46
aerobic capacity, benefits of improving 158-159
aerobic endurance 149
ages for participation in international competitions 14t
agonist muscles 95
anaerobic endurance 149
anatomical adaptation 96
anatomical age
    athletic development, third phase (most important) 12
    factors affecting 10, 12
    growth and development 10
    stages of 11t
antagonist muscles 94-95
Armstrong 157
athletic age
    difficulty in determining 14
    long-term training plans, importance in designing 14
athletic development, initiation stage (6 to 10 years old)
    in flexibility program 33
    guidelines for training programs 23-25
    physical and psychological considerations 23
athletic development, stages of
    about 21-22, 23
    athletic formation (11 to 14 years old) 25-26
    high performance (19 years old and over) 28
    initiation stage (6 to 10 years old) 23-25
    specialization (15 to 18 years old) 26-28
athletic formation (11 to 14 years old)
    about 25, 45-46
    guidelines for designing training programs 25-26

average age of participants at the Olympic Games between 1968 and 1992 29t

B

Bailey 64, 65, 98, 154
balance 43
ballistic training 73
Bar-Or 94, 97
base heart rate (BHR) 177, 179
Bell 32
biological age
    assessing capabilities of athletes with 13
    defined 12-13
    in sports champions, examples of 13
Bompa 94, 97
Borms 100
Bowers 97

C

Ceapura, L. 13
chronological age, in sports programs, misuse of 13
circuit training
    about 101-102
    for early postpuberty 112t
    for early postpuberty (more challenging) 112t
    nine exercises 101
    with nine exercises 103t
    six exercises 101
    with six exercises 102t
Comaneci, Nadia 13
comparison between early specialization and multilateral development 4t
competition, excelling in
    about 167
    nutrition for training and competition 172-173
    problems with 167-168, 169-171
    readiness for 174-175
    stress and burnout, preventing 175-176
    training, monitoring 176-178

competition, problems with
  about 167-168
  competing too early 168, 169
  competing too often 169
  injuries, risk of 171
  late maturing children, discrimination
      against 171
  skill development, emphasizing 170-171
competitions for children, suggested
      types and number of 172t
concentration and willpower 72
Coop 175
coordination training
  about 46-47, 49, 50
  when to start 43

D
Davies 157
Docherty 32
Duda 98

E
early postpuberty, strength exercises for
    132-139
early postpuberty, training program for 111
early specialization and multilateral devel-
    opment, comparison between 4t
Eastern European sports schools, about 3
endurance training
  about 149-150
  adaptation of children's organs and
      systems for 150
  athletic formation phase, consider-
      ations for 153-155, 156-157
  benefits of 149
  exercises for postpuberty 165
  fatigue 149
  genetics and influence of other factors
      on 150
  health benefits of 150
  initiation phase (prepuberty), consider-
      ations for 151-152, 153
    about 151
  initiation phase (prepuberty), consid-
      erations for
    program design 152, 153
  initiation phase (prepuberty), consider-
      ations for
    scope of 151-152
  performance ability 150
  specialization phase, considerations for
      157-159
  team sports 150
  types of 149

endurance training, athletic formation
      phase, considerations for
  about 153-154
  program design 155, 156
  scope of 154-155
  training program 156-157
endurance training, considerations for
      specialization phase
  about 157
  endurance training, scope of 158
  program design 158-159
  scope of 158
endurance training exercises for prepu-
      berty
  controlled speed polygon 160
  off into nature 162
  off into nature (variation of) 162
  quad 161
  square 161
endurance training exercises for puberty
  aerobic technical run 163
  interval training runs 164
  long repetitions for pace judgment 163
  10-minute triangle run 164
  passing on the right 165
ergogenesis 158
exercise, benefits of 151
exercises and skills, about 50
external resistance, ability to overcome
      72

F
Falkel 100
fixators (stabilizers) 95
Fleck 98, 99, 100
flexibility, periodization of 34
flexibility exercises
  ankle double touch 37
  ankle stretch 39
  diagonal ankle press 40
  double kicks 40
  flex to opposite leg 36
  hamstring stretch 38
  hurdle stretch 39
  large body circles 36
  opposite toe touches 38
  partner hamstring stretch 42
  partner shoulder stretch 41
  scale stretch 42
  sea lion stretch 40
  seated hip flexions 41
  seated toe touch 37
  shoulder bow stretch 39
  standing shoulder stretch 41

straddle medicine ball rotations 38
straddle stretch 37
trunk and hip flexion 36
flexibility program during initiation
    stage, designing 33
flexibility training
    about 31
    developing 32
    exercises 36-42
    periodization model for 35t
    program, designing 33-34
    progression for 35t
    stretching, methods of 32-33
Foss 97
Fox 97
free weights, training with 109

G
game, duration of (for prepuberty) 66
gender differences in running speed 64
Goldberg 94, 97
growth plate injuries 100

H
Hanson 175
Harre 4
Hebbelinck 64, 100, 151
high performance stage 22
high performance (19 years old and over),
    about 28
high starts, performing 72, 73
Higson, Allison 13
Hirtz 46
Howe, Gordie 13
how training elements increase in the
    step method 19t
Hughson 150, 153

I
individual characteristics, understanding
    about 10
    ages for participation in international
        competitions 14t
    anatomical age 10, 11t, 12
    athletic age 14
    athletic development, third phase 12
    biological age 12-13
    climate and altitude, influences of 10,
        12
    stages of anatomical age 11t
    step loading 17-18, 19
    strengths and limitations 10
injuries, preventing 100-101
injury-prevention techniques 101

J
Jordan, Michael 1

K
Kraemer 98, 99

L
laws of strength training
    about 95
    developing core strength before limbs
        96-97
    developing joint flexibility 96
    developing tendon strength before
        muscle strength 96
linear acceleration 185
long-term ratio between specific and
    multilateral development 6t
lung functioning 151

M
Malina 64, 65, 98, 100, 154
Matsuda 102
Matsui 97, 150
maturation, early and late 171
methodology for training 105
Micheli 97, 98
microcycle for a team sport athlete 75t
microcycle (weekly) training plan for an
    individual sport to develop maxi-
    mum acceleration 75t
Mirwald 64, 65, 99
motor skills, periodization model for 47t-
    49t
motor skills exercises
    backroll into a handstand 60
    backward rolling 54
    behind overhead throw 55
    between-leg throw 55
    cartwheel 55
    coordination for limbs 53
    dodge game 59
    foot dribble 52
    front somersault 51
    handstand 60
    jump and roll with turn 61
    overhand simultaneous throw 56
    overhand throw relay 57
    overhand zigzag and target throw 57
    over the net game (volleyball court) 58
    rebounding ball catch 56
    rolling target 58
    roll with turns 60
    scissors-kick handstand 54
    skipping rope 53

motor skills exercises (continued)
   target kick 52
   throw, roll, and catch 61
   two-hand chest and overhead pass 56
   utility ball dribbling 51
   v-sit balance 59
   walking the plank 62
motor skills training
   about 43-44
   athletic formation, considerations for
      45-46
   designing a program 46-47, 49, 50
   exercises 51—62
   exercises and skills, about 50
   initiation, considerations for 44-45
   specialization, considerations for 46
movement time 63, 72
multilateral and specialized phase of
      training, about 22
multilateral development
   about 3
   compared with early specialization 4
   Eastern European sports schools 3
   purpose of 4
   skills, developing a variety of 3
   in a well-rounded sports program 4
multilateral development, purpose of 4
multilateral development and specialized
      training for different ages, ratio
      between 6f
multilateral phase, purpose of 22
multilateral process, understanding 44
multilateral training and advanced
      athletes, example of 5
multilateral training program
   benefits of 4
   longitudinal study of 4, 5
muscle elasticity 72
muscle overload 100
muscular endurance 94

N

Nagorni 4
nutrition for training and competition
   dehydration 172
   food guide pyramid 172, 173f
   postpuberty, athletes at 173
   prepuberty, athletes at 172
   puberty, athletes at 172, 173

P

periodization
   about 22
   for an annual plan for early postpu-
      berty 166t

of endurance training for an annual
      plan with two competitive phases
      (late postpuberty) 166t
of long-term training 21-22, 22f
model for endurance training for
      prepuberty 153t
model for endurance training for
      puberty 155t
model for motor skills 47t-49t
model for endurance training for
      postpuberty 160t
model for speed training for late
      postpuberty 79t
model for speed training for postpu-
      berty 73t, 77t
model for speed training for postpu-
      berty for a team sport 80t
model for speed training prepuberty
      67t
model for strength training for annual
      plan for late postpuberty 113t
*Periodization: Theory and Methodology of
   Training* (Bompa) 28
Periodization Training for Sports (Bompa)
   28
play-specific speed 64
postpuberty and strength training
   about 98-100
   early maturing boys 100
   early maturing girls 99
postpubescence and speed training
   about 68, 69, 70, 71
   program for 71-72, 73-74, 76, 78
power 94
power development, training program for
   113t
prepuberty, sample workout for 49t
prepuberty, strength exercises for 116-
   124
prepuberty and developing coordination
   44-45
prepuberty and speed training
   about 64
   program for 65-66
prepuberty and strength training 98
prepubescence 151
prepubescent speed development
   about 64
   drills 65
   improving program for 65-66
prime movers 94
puberty, strength exercises for 124-132
puberty, strength gains 67
puberty and speed training 68, 69, 70
puberty and strength training 98

pubescence and coordination abilities 45-46

R

Ramsay 97
reaction time, improving 68
relays for speed training 66
repetitions, number of 95
rigidity 71
Roberts 151
Rotella 175
Rovere 100
running form technique, about 69f
running step, phases of 69f

S

Sale 97
sample workout for prepuberty 49t
Sampras, Pete 1
Sharma 46
Shephard 151, 153, 157
skill formation, phases of 184
skills, developing a variety of 3
Smith 98
specialization
    about 6
    training, exercises to include 6
    when to start 8-9
specialization, guidelines for the road to 7t-8t
specialization and coordination in adolescence 46
specialization stage
    about 22
    and flexibility 34
specialization (15 to 18 years old)
    about 26
    guidelines for designing training programs 26-28
specificity of training, suggested long-term approach to 3f
specificity training, problems with 2-3
specifity training
    injuries from 10
    starting too early, problems from 2-3
speed
    about 63, 72
    elements of 63
speed and movement time exercises 68, 69
speed development during puberty 66, 67-68
speed drills, about 64-65
speed endurance 73, 74
speed gains, benefits of 70, 71

speed tasks and skill performance (for speed training), combining 66
speed training
    about 63-64
    athletic formation, model for 66, 67-68, 69-70
    distance, increasing progressively 66
    drill, duration of 65
    and high performance 71
    initiation, model for 64-66
    and postpubescence 68, 69, 71
    program design 65-66
    rest interval between repetitions 69-70
    scope of 64-65, 68
    specialization, model for 70, 71-72, 73-74, 76, 78
    for sprinting 185-186
speed training, exercises and skills
    acceleration run 85
    arm swing drill 83
    backward crossover 90
    beanbag relay 85
    beanbag shuttle 86
    big steps 84
    carioca 90
    falling start 83
    file relay 81
    finders keepers 87
    foot touches 91
    forward crossover 89
    fox and squirrel 82
    go, go, go, stop 91
    harness running 85
    high knees 84
    loop, the 86
    low obstacle relay 89
    obstacle course 88
    octopus tag 82
    partner tag 82
    quick steps 84
    rabbits and roosters 87
    slalom relay 81
    standing start drills 83
    tents and campers 88
speed training during puberty 68
speed training for late postpuberty, periodization model for 79t
speed training for postpuberty, periodization model for 73t, 77t
speed training for postpuberty for a team sport, periodization model for 80t
speed training for prepuberty, periodization model 67t
speed training for puberty, periodization model for 70t

speed training model for athletic forma-
        tion
    about 66, 67-68
    program design 68, 69-70
    scope of 68
speed training model for initiation
    about 64
    program design 65-66
    scope of 64-65
speed training model for specialization
    about 70, 71
    program design 71-72, 73-74, 76, 78
    scope of 71
speed training session 67t
speed training with sport-specific forms 73
sports, reasons for dropping out of 169
sprinting speed 74, 76
stages of anatomical age 11t
starts 185
step loading
    using 17-18
step method 17-18, 19, 20
step method, how training elements
        increase in 19t
strains, sprains and soft tissue damage
        100-101
strength and power training
    about 93-94
    athletic formation phase, model for
        104-108
    benefits of 93-94
    circuit training 101-102
    defined 93
    early post-puberty, training program
        for 111-112
    exercises for early postpuberty 131-137
    exercises for late postpuberty 138-147
    exercises for postpuberty 131-147
    exercises for prepuberty 115-123
    exercises for puberty 123-131
    getting ready for 94
    initiation phase, model for 104
    injuries, preventing 100-101
    late postpuberty, training program for
        113, 114
    laws of 95-97
    misconceptions of 93
    number of repetitions, guidelines for 95
    readiness for 94
    specialization phase, model for 108,
        109, 110-111
    terminology 94-95
    for young athletes, adapting 97-100

strength gains 97
strength training, adapting for young
        athletes
    about 97
    postpuberty, considerations for 98-100
    prepuberty, considerations for 97
    puberty, considerations for 98
    training per week during the season,
        structure of 19t
strength training, laws of
    developing core strength before limbs
        96-97
    developing joint flexibility 96
    developing tendon strength before
        muscle strength 96
strength training exercises for early
        postpuberty
    abdominal rainbows 135
    about 132
    arm curls 135
    baseball or tennis ball throws for
        accuracy 139
    cable triceps (elbow) extensions 134
    chest press 133
    cone jumps 138
    continuous squat jumps 138
    half squats 137
    incline bench sit-ups 135
    lats pull down (front) 134
    leg curls 136
    leg press 136
    push-up progression 133
    reverse leg press 136
    scissors splits 137
    shoulder press 134
    slalom jumps 137
    vertical hops 138
    v-sits 135
strength training exercises for late post-
        puberty
    abdominal arches 142
    abdominal thrusts 142
    back kicks 145
    back roll into handstand 146
    back roll into vertical jump 146
    caterpillar push-ups 140
    dipping 141
    double-leg medicine ball forward toss
        143
    drop push-ups 141
    forward roll and vertical jump 145
    inclined overhead leg lifts 142
    knee-tuck jumps 144

medicine ball speed throws 148
medicine ball volleyball game 148
obstacle relay 147
pull-ups 140
rope climbs 140
rope push-ups 147
seated pull-ups 139
thrust legs upward 144
trunk extensions 143
wall push-ups 141
strength training exercises for prepuberty
abdominal crunches 120
chest raises and clap 121
dodge the rope 123
dumbbell curls 116
dumbbell flys 117
dumbbell overhead raises 117
dumbbell shoulder press 116
dumbbell side raises 116
loop skips 122
medicine ball back roll 120
medicine ball chest throws 118
medicine ball scoop throw 119
medicine ball side pass relay 124
medicine ball standing overhead
throws 119
medicine ball twist throws 118
seated back extensions 121
single-leg back raises 121
trunk twists 120
two-leg skips 122
zigzag medicine ball throws 123
strength training exercises for puberty
about 124
baseball or tennis dart game 132
between-leg backward overhead shot
throw 126
between-leg forward shot/medicine
ball throw 127
between-leg medicine ball backward
throw 128
clap push-ups 125
double-leg side lifts 128
hang hip flexion 127
hip thrusts 127
large medicine ball sit-up throws 128
medicine ball backward throws 129
medicine ball chest pass relay 130
medicine ball trunk raises 129
obstacle run relay 131
over-under bridge relay 130
push-ups 125
roll medicine ball under the bridge 131

single-leg burpees 125
trunk raised medicine ball throws 129
two-handed medicine ball side throw
126
strength training for annual plan for late
postpuberty, periodization model for
113t
strength training (long-term),
periodization model for 114t
strength training model for athletic
formation phase
about 104-108
program design 105
training, scope of 105
training program 106
strength training model for initiation
phase 104
strength training model for specialization
phase
about 108
circuit training with 12 exercises 103t
program design 108-111
scope of training 108
training program 110
strength training program, progression of
95
strength training program for maximum
strength 114t
stress and burnout, preventing
suggestions for athletes 175-176
suggestions for coaches 176
stretching, methods of
ballistic stretching 32-33
proprioceptive neuromuscular facilitation (PNF) 32, 33
static stretching 32
when to perform 31
synergist (agonists) muscles 94-95

T
Takemoto, M. 13
team sports and speed training 66
technique 72
training, defined 1
training, monitoring
about 176, 177
heart rate chart 177-178, 179, 180
psychological traits and appetite chart
178, 181, 182
training guidelines
about 1-2
individual characteristics, understanding 10, 12-13

training guidelines (continued)
  program, developing a long-term 2-3, 4, 5, 6, 8-9
  training load, increasing appropriately 15-16, 17-18, 19
  variety, adding 9-10
training load
  for a four-week cycle, increase of 18f
  during the season 19
  for a three-week cycle, increase of 18f
training load, increasing appropriately 15-16
  exercises, number of 16
  gradual increase, benefits of 15
  progression of training session length for a soccer team 16t
  step loading 17-18, 19
  training, weeks and months of 17
  training sessions, duration and frequency of 16
  understanding methods used 15
training log 114t
training models for various sports, long-term
  baseball 189
  basketball 190
  football 191
  gymnastics (women) 192
  ice hockey 193
  soccer 194
  swimming 195
  tennis 196
  track and field, sprinting 187
  track and field, throws and jumps 188
  volleyball 197
training per week during the season, structure of 19t
training plans, long-term, about 183-186
training program, developing a long-term
  about 2-3
  appropriate specificity of training, suggested long-term 3f
  early specialization and multilateral development, comparisons 4t
  multilateral development 3, 4, 5

specialization, guidelines for 7t-8t
specialized development 6, 8-9
training program for late postpuberty
  strength, training program for each type of 113
training programs
  considerations for children 23
  dynamics of growth and development for each stage, considering 100
  evaluation of 1-2
  long-term development for athlete 1
  most effective 19
training session(s)
  areas to progressively increase 16
  length for a soccer team, progression of 16t
  and weather conditions 16
training variety, adding
  about 9-10
  importance 9
  injuries 10
  repetitive training, problems with 9
  too much 10

U

upper-body movement time (speed training), improving 66
upper-body power, gains in during puberty 67-68

W

weekly schedule with four training sessions 177
weekly schedule with three training sessions 176
weights, lifting heavy 100
weight training 104
Wood, Murray 13

Y

Yeu, A. 13

Z

Zatopek, Emil 150

About the Author

Tudor Bompa is recognized worldwide as the foremost expert on periodization training—conditioning programs that balance the loads, lengths, and intensities of workouts for maximum performance. He first developed the concept of "periodization of strength" in Romania in 1963, as he helped the eastern bloc countries rise to dominance in the athletic world. Since then, Bompa has used his system to train 11 Olympic Games medalists, and periodization training has become a standard method for conditioning champion athletes.

A full professor at York University in Toronto, Bompa has authored several important books on physical conditioning, including *Serious Strength Training* (Human Kinetics, 1998); *Periodization: Theory and Methodology of Training* (Human Kinetics, 1999); *Periodization Training for Sports* (Human Kinetics, 1999); and *Power Training for Sport: Plyometrics for Maximum Power Development*; as well as numerous articles on the subject. His work has been translated into nine languages, and he has made presentations on training theories, planning, and periodization in more than 30 countries. His publications, conferences, and ideas are highly regarded and enthusiastically sought after by many top professional athletes and training specialists. Bompa lives in Sharon, Ontario.

Bompa currently offers a certification program in training, planning, and periodization called "The Tudor Bompa Training System." The program is designed for personal trainers, instructors, coaches, athletes, and educators. For more information, contact Dr. Tudor Bompa, P.O. Box 95, Sharon, ON, L0G 1V0, Canada.